SHIPMINDER
The Story of Her Majesty's Coastguard

SHIPMINDER
The story of Her Majesty's Coastguard

Bernard Scarlett

 PELHAM BOOKS

First published in Great Britain by
PELHAM BOOKS LTD
52 Bedford Square
London, W.C.1
1971

7207 0480 4

Set and printed in Great Britain by
Bristol Typesetting Co Ltd,
Barton Manor, St Philips, Bristol
in Plantin eleven on twelve point on
paper supplied by P. E. Bingham Ltd,
and bound by the Dorstel Press

For Fred Keating
in memoriam

Contents

Foreword by Sir Max Aitken, Bart, DSO, DFC   11

Author's Note   13

Introduction   15

1   The Bad Old Days   19

2   The Coast Blockade   30

3   Birth of the Coastguard   43

4   Great Gun Exercise   58

5   Gubby Ships and Hulks   70

6   Signallers and Life-savers   81

7   Public Opinion to the Rescue   94

8   The Coastguard Goes to War   106

9   The Coastguard has its 'Troubles'   117

10   Under New Management   128

11   The Loss of the *Islander*   140

12   To War Again   155

13   The Modern Coastguard Service   171

14   Afloat Again   191

Index   203

Illustrations

	facing page
'Saved' drawn by J. D. Watson 1866	32
Ceremonial Funeral 1891	32
Pistol Firing Practice	33
Portable Searchlight for Cliff Rescue	33
Typical Cliff Rescue	64
Wreck of the *Jeanne Gougy*	64
Saved from *Jeanne Gougy*	65
Trawler *Summerside* ashore Aberdeenshire	65
Trawler *Grenada* aground Suffolk	96
Crewman Helped Ashore from *Grenada*	96
Torrey Canyon oil leak	97
Torrey Canyon after the bombing	97
U.S. Coast Guard Cutter *Vigilant*	128
Cliff-top Rendezvous	128
Modern Coastguard Rescue H.Q. Deal	129
Coastguards on Look-out	129

Acknowledgements

Thanks are due to the following for permission to reproduce the illustrations.
1, South Shields Volunteer Life Brigade; 2, District Officer Pawson of Deal; 3, W. Eglon Shaw; 4, Central Office of Information; 5, Aberdeen Journal; 6 and 7, Western Morning News; 8, Scottish Daily Express; 9 and 10, Eastern Daily Press; 11 and 12, Press Association; 13, U.S. Coast Guard; 14, Ministry of Defence (Air); 15 and 16, Department of Trade and Industry.
A*

Foreword
by
Sir Max Aitken, Bart, DSO, DFC

All those who go afloat owe a considerable debt to the Coast-guard Service.

The meticulous way in which the Service is run and organized should be an example and a lesson to all small boat owners and sailors.

Often not enough care is taken in such vital matters as safety navigation and seamanship.

Haphazard preparation leads to endless time, trouble and often risk when forethought could have prevented accidents, gear failure and even drowning.

All yachtsmen should salute this magnificent Service and be happy in the knowledge that the Coastguards are always on the lookout.

Max Aitken

Author's Note

I must record my gratitude to the many people without whose help and encouragement this book would not have been written.

Firstly, the man whose enthusiasm for the subject was my inspiration – Frederick Keating of the Board of Trade, his sudden death on the eve of publication of the first issue under his Editorship of *The Coastguard* magazine, deprived the Coastguard Service of its most ardent propagandist.

I am grateful to Commander John Douglas, M.B.E., R.N. (Retd) Chief Inspector of Coastguard, and his predecessor Commander P. J. H. Bartlett, O.B.E., R.N.(Retd) who provided official reports and a wealth of valuable advice; to Mr E. Carson, Librarian and Archivist of H.M. Customs & Excise for allowing me access to eighteenth and nineteenth-century Customs records; to Miss V. Reilly of the Admiralty Archives Library for assembling and advising on pre-1914 records; the staff of the Board of Trade Marine Division archives for making wartime material available; Mr R. Barlow, Editor of *The Coastguard* for arranging my visits to Coastguard Stations and the District Officers and their staffs who patiently answered my questions; and to the officials of the Public Record Office without whose expert advice the unearthing of relevant documents would have been impossible.

I am also indebted to Commander C. A. de W. Kitcat, M.B.E., R.N.(Retd), for allowing me to make use of material from his many excellent articles on the Volunteer Brigades of the North East Coast, and, the history of life-saving rockets.

Books I have consulted:

Smuggling Days and Smuggling Ways by Lieut. The Hon. Henry N. Shore (1892)

H.M. Coastguard by Frank Bowen (1927)

Historical Notes on the Coastguard Service 1907, H.M.S.O.

Introduction

The invasion was imminent, eyes scanned the sea from the cliff-tops, as they had for a hundred and fifty years – the eyes of Britain's first line of defence against smugglers and the elements, Her Majesty's Coastguard.

It was the Spring of 1967, and as cabinet ministers conferred, the army, navy, and air force stood-to, scientists worked round the clock testing new weapons, and the black enemy floated inexorably towards the coasts of Devon and Cornwall.

The men of the Coastguard, the intelligence corps without whose reports no battle plan could be formulated, were in the thick of the biggest and dirtiest invasion ever seen on our coasts – the oil slick from the *Torrey Canyon*.

The work of the service rarely makes the newspaper headlines, but to 'they that go down to the sea in ships; that do business in great waters', and, to the others who merely go down to the seaside to mess about in boats or on the beaches, the work of the Coastguard is vital.

Stations and look-outs, strategically sited, keep constant visual and radio-listening watch for ships in distress, ready to turn out skilled teams to save lives from shipwrecks and accidents round the 6,000 miles of coastline of the United Kingdom.

With the unprecedented boom in the sailing of small boats, often by inexperienced sailors, the Service becomes more essential each year.

Emergencies at sea can quickly lead to catastrophe. It may be as calm as a millpond when the sails of a dinghy are set to catch the slightest zephyr, but let a sudden squall blow and the green sailor can find his craft out of control. It is then that the trained Coastguardsman becomes the guardian angel.

He may spot trouble from his look-out post, or receive a '999' emergency telephone call alerting him to the danger. It is the Coastguard who sets in motion the whole gamut of rescue- and life-saving operations. He may call out the lifeboat, ask for assistance from a helicopter air-sea rescue unit of the Royal Navy or R.A.F., or request longer sea searches by aircraft when a 'Mayday' or 'S.O.S.' message is picked up indicating that a ship is in danger.

It is the duty officer at the coastguard station who must use his knowledge and training to decide which form of rescue operation is required.

Having set the wheels in motion, he becomes the vital link between the rescue organizations, receiving reports and co-ordinating operations.

The coastguardsman is no passive onlooker of the dramas of the sea, as the work of the lifesaving companies shows. The men of these teams turn out hundreds of times every year and, often at great risk to themselves; in the worst possible conditions of foul weather; in darkness; dense fog and blinding snowstorms; stumbling across ice-covered rocks; they set up the breeches-buoy apparatus and snatch the shipwrecked from certain death or injury.

In the drowsy heat of a high summer day, when holidaymakers crowd the beaches and cliffs, the coastguard is fully alert to the hidden dangers to the unwary and foolhardy. He listens for cries for help from the inexperienced climber who challenging an unfamiliar cliff finds he is over-ambitious, loses his nerve and is unable to go forward or retreat. His cry will bring the coastguard cliff-rescue team to the scene. If a child ventures too close to a cliff edge, falls and lies injured, or, as has happened, a flock of sheep follow their leader off a cliff, the rescue team will be on hand with special equipment.

The call could be to sunbathers cut off by a rising tide, when the swift arrival of a helicopter or lifeboat can avert tragedy.

Not every day brings a shipwreck or cliff rescue, the weather even in Britain is not always foul, but blue skies and calm seas bring little relaxation to the men of the Service. The section of Coastguard Regulations headed Index of Miscellaneous Duties makes certain that they are second to none for sheer versatility.

Coastguards help with the training of lifeboat men in signalling procedures. They keep weather observations for the Air Ministry and supply meteorological reports.

They are responsible for the general supervision of the foreshore and must report encroachments.

The men of the Service must be experts in the identification of sea-creatures, and are responsible for the disposal of carcasses washed ashore. In certain cases they must remove the lower jaw-bone of the dead creature and after cleaning it, send it to the Natural History Museum in Kensington.

Coastguards assist with the administration of the Wild Birds Act, and, in their spare time (*sic*) they must watch for any movement of navigational marks.

These are but a few of the multifarious jobs which, throughout its history, have been foisted on the willing Coastguard Service by various Government Departments, happy to hive off unwanted duties but ever reluctant to accept responsibility for financing the Service.

In both world wars the Coastguards kept watch for attempts to land spies or saboteurs from enemy vessels.

During the 'Troubles' in Ireland in the 1920s the men of the Coastguard and their Stations bore the brunt of terrorist attacks. They withstood sieges and armed raids, their posts were blown sky-high, their homes and personal property destroyed, they endured the sullen hostility of the populace, by whom they were regarded as the representatives of imperialist Britain.

The Service owes its existence to the deprecations of the eighteenth and nineteenth-century freetraders, as smugglers were called.

It formed the first Royal Naval Reserve which replaced the infamous impressment or press-gang method of recruitment to the senior service.

In spite of this records tell of tedious arguments between Government Departments about its role. For most of its existence there was insufficient money to meet the needs of the Service. Disbanded, reformed, control shuffled from one Department to another – and worse – split between two or more branches of Government, subject to carping criticism and searching Committees of Inquiry, always an early victim of economy campaigns in peace-time, and depleted of manpower in war, the Coastguard has survived.

With its morale high and pride in its history, the Service has weathered the political storms and, under the mantle of the Marine Division of the Board of Trade – the telegraphic address of which was appropriately 'Shipminder, London' – it has developed into a great life-saving service in which men are proud to serve.

It is to the modern Coastguard that this book is dedicated.

Chaldon.

Bernard Scarlett

I
The Bad Old Days

It is remarkable that at the end of the 17th and beginning of the 18th century no organization existed which was capable of preventing freetraders from landing huge masses of illicit goods, more or less unimpeded, on the shores of the southern counties of England.

In time of war little was done to prevent the free passage of enemy spies or the export of gold to finance the enemy's war effort.

It was the Emperor Napoleon who, when in exile on St Helena, revealed that much of the cash he raised to pay for his military campaigns came, albeit unknowingly, from the merchants and bankers in the Capital of his foe—the City of London.

'I did not receive money direct from Spain. I got bills on Vera Cruz which certain agents sent by circuitous routes, by Amsterdam, Hamburg and other places to London, as I had no direct communication' the Emperor boasted. 'The bills were discounted by merchants in London to whom ten per cent and sometimes a premium was paid as their reward. Bills were then given by them upon different bankers in Europe for the greatest part of the amount, and the remainder in gold, which last was brought over to France by the smugglers.

'Even for the equipping of my last expedition, after my return from Elba, a great part of the money was raised in London' he claimed.

Not only did the smugglers carry gold to the Emperor, they also ran huge quantities of illicit goods from France at a time when the Royal Navy was imposing a strict coastal blockade aimed at strangling the enemy's trade. With complete lack of patriotism they carried dispatches between Napoleon and his agents, and sometimes the spies themselves.

'They did great mischief to your government. They took from France annually 40 or 50 millions in silks and brandy,' Napoleon said, speaking of the smugglers. 'During the war they had a part of Dunkirk allotted to them, to which they were restricted but as they latterly went out of their limits, committed riots, and insulted everybody, I ordered Gravelines to be prepared for their reception where they had a little camp for their accommodation. At one time there were upwards of 500 of them in Dunkirk.'

So valuable were the deprecations of the freetraders to the French war effort that no attempt was made to molest them although they were enemy aliens and should at least have been interned.

It may have been alarm at the complete lack of effective security which finally forced the government to take action in 1809, but there was also the pressure of public opinion from the populations of towns and villages on and near the south coast where the smuggling bands roamed at will.

For many years the smuggler had been a romantic figure and the goods he 'ran' were in great demand by all classes because of rising prices.

The Customs organization was completely ineffectual and often corrupt, and efforts by the government to clamp down on the freetraders met with little success and served merely to brutalize them.

In 1719 an Act was passed making parties of eight or more smugglers liable to transportation, but when this failed to suppress the gangs the figure was reduced to five. However the law had the reverse effect to that intended. At the height of their activities, in the mid-1700s, smugglers were running goods openly along the entire seaboard of the United Kingdom.

Mr Henry Baker, the Supervisor for Kent and Sussex, in his report to Custom House, London in December 1703 declared: For fine goods, as they call them, (silks, laces etc.) I am well assured that trade goes on through both counties, though not in such vast quantities as have been formerly brought in – I mean in those days when (as a gentleman of estate in one of the counties has written this twelvemonth, told me) he had been once, besides at other times at the landing of a waggon with silks, lace etc., till six oxen could hardly move it out of the place.

In the next forty years the smugglers, in large bands, rode through the countryside, armed with guns and clubs, forcing the good people of the villages to stand facing the walls of their houses so that they could truthfully say they did not see the free-traders pass.

In the 1730s tea had become the principal item of smuggled merchandise. In 1736 a petition was presented to parliament by the tea-traders asserting that nearly half the tea consumed in the country had paid no duty.

A pamphlet *A Proposal for Preventing of Running Goods*, published in December 1743 claimed that 'Since an excise of 4/od per pound was laid on tea it has brought an average of £160,000 a year into the Exchequer, which is but for 650,000 lbs weight of tea. But real consumption is vastly greater. Some years ago the treasurers of our East India Company received a letter from Holland intimating that one person in the province of Zeeland smuggled yearly for England no less than half a million pounds. The directors upon enquiring were convinced that there was such a person who, some years before had been but an English sailor, was now married to a woman that kept a china shop, and had so well managed affairs that he had four sloops of his own constantly employed in smuggling; that the quantity of tea he was supposed to export had not at all been magnified, and that he had more guineas and English specie in his house than any banker in England.'

The consumption of tea throughout Britain at that time had been computed to be about one and a half million pounds, which sold from bond at 5/9d to 6/10d per lb.

Tales of smuggling have a romantic appeal to the modern reader with glamorised stories of fights with the excisemen, but a closer look at this aspect of those far-off days shows there was little glamour and much terrorism, brutality and sadistic murder.

The excisemen, revenue officers and 'riding officers' were natural targets for attack, and these unfortunate men could expect no help from the local populace who themselves went in dread of reprisals.

None of the maritime counties was without its gang of smugglers and the range of their goods was large. If it was not brandy or silk or wine, it was tea or cinnamon, Holland's gin, in fact anything which had a ready sale to the public if it could be had without payment of Customs dues.

There were land smugglers and sea smugglers; the latter brought their goods in their own ships or off-loaded them from foreign vessels and landed them on the coast. These men were the bold reckless characters who have, perhaps with some justification, become the romantic figures of history.

The others – the land smugglers – were gangs of desperadoes, well armed and mounted, who carried the smuggled goods from the coast to the interior for distribution to the 'retailers'.

Every inn was supported by smugglers who received help in return. Scarcely a house near the coast did not have a place for concealing goods. Even churchyards became repositories for kegs of spirits and bales of cloth, and, with the willing help of the sexton the churches and their vaults were excellent hiding places. Not that the parsons were unaware that their churches often contained spirits other than those of the dead, and it has been said that the brandy punch at the home of many a village pastor was of exceedingly high quality.

In Kent and Sussex the most notorious smugglers band was known as the Hawkhurst Gang. These were brutal ruffians who indulged in every kind of atrocity. Their repeated attacks and cruelty finally exasperated the good people of Goudhurst who determined to end the domination which had become intolerable.

A young man of the village named Sturt, who had served with the army, drew up a declaration expressing the determination of the inhabitants to oppose the smugglers. This was signed by a considerable number of villagers who banded together to form the Goudhurst Militia, under Sturt's leadership. Soon after the formation of the militia one of the villagers was captured by the Hawkhurst Gang. He was tortured until he revealed the intentions of his companions and was sent back to the village with a message calculated to strike fear into the population. The gang would attack the place, murder all the inhabitants and burn the village to the ground.

Sturt's men threw up hasty defences, scoured the surrounding countryside for weapons and melted down all the available lead to make ball-shot for their muskets.

As they had promised, the gang armed to the teeth and led by a man called Thomas Kingsmill descended on the village. After shouting bloodcurdling threats they opened fire. The militia returned the fusillade killing two of the smugglers and wounding several others. The villagers' resistance put the gang to flight.

The escapade for which Thomas Kingsmill was later executed was an attack on the Custom House at Poole, Dorset, in which the Hawkhurst Gang seized thirty-seven hundredweights of tea, in, what the prosecution later described as 'the most unheard-of act of villainy and impudence ever known'.

It happened like this: The tea had been seized by a revenue cutter from Poole after a ship had been intercepted and captured. The cargo was deposited in the King's Warehouse, as the Custom House was called.

The smugglers, sixty strong and well armed, gathered in Charlton Forest and split into two parties. One was sent to attack the warehouse while the men of the other party were posted on roads leading to Poole to watch for the movement of troops.

During the night of 6th–7th October 1747, the gang broke into the warehouse, loaded the tea onto pack-horses, and next day rode in broad daylight through Fordingbridge with their loot. Hundreds of people saw them pass but more than eighteen months passed before any arrests were made.

A reward was offered for information, but it was a chance word overheard at Fordingbridge which gave the authorities the first clue to the gang.

A witness was found who was prepared to testify, but to strike terror into the populace he and his escort were to become the victims of barbarous murders.

On a Sunday morning in February 1748, four months after the raid, a Fordingbridge shoemaker named Chater, and an elderly tide-waiter named Galley employed by Customs at Southampton, rode up to the White Hart Inn at Stanstead, carrying with them a letter from Major Batten, a Justice of the Peace for Sussex.

Their arrival roused the suspicions of the innkeeper, the Widow Payne, who had two smuggler sons. The widow sent for her offspring and told them that she suspected the visitors were likely to harm the smugglers.

The news of the strangers' presence quickly spread and the leaders of the smugglers hurried to the inn. After a few drinks, one of them induced Chater to accompany him outside and there he soon obtained confirmation of the widow's suspicions. The shoemaker was on his way to swear information against one of the Hawkhurst Gang concerned in the raid at Poole.

Chater returned to the bar and, plied with drinks by their new-found friends, he and Galley soon fell drunk to the floor and were carried to bed. In the middle of the night the still drunken men were taken to the inn yard and tied onto one horse and were led away. It was at first intended to deport the men to France – a favourite method of smugglers to dispose of inquisitive excise men – but the wives of the gang provoked their men by shouting 'hang the dogs, they came to hang us'.

It was then decided to keep the prisoners in a secret hideout until the authorities had made up their minds on the action they would take against the smuggler who had been arrested on suspicion, and against whom Chater was on his way to give evidence.

However, the cavalcade had no sooner started from the inn than the leader, a smuggler named Jackson, began to whip the prisoners, shouting 'whip them, cut them, slash them, damn them'. The entire gang then set about the unfortunate men with brutal ferocity, cutting them across their faces, heads and shoulders with long whips until they rolled over the horse's back and hung with their heads between its hooves.

Early in the morning the gang arrived at the village of Rake, near Liss, where the landlord of the Red Lion was persuaded to admit them. After another drinking bout, Galley was dragged out to a nearby wood and was buried alive in a sandpit.

While Galley was being disposed of, Chater, blood streaming from his wounds, was taken to the house of a well-known smuggler at Trotton, a village about four miles away. There he was chained to the doorpost of an outhouse and was left for two days and nights while his demise was plotted. It was decided that he should be shot but this was discarded as 'shooting was too quick a death to be a terror to all such informing rogues for the future'. It was then agreed that he should be hurled down Harris's Well in Lady Holt Park.

An attempt was made to hang Chater at the well but the rope was too short and left the body hanging half over the edge. The rope was released and Chater hurled headfirst into the well. The smugglers then rained stones and pieces of timber down on him until they were sure he was dead.

The first clue to the brutal murders was the discovery of Galley's bloodstained greatcoat on the road near Rowland's Castle, and a Proclamation was issued offering a reward and free pardon to anyone who should discover what had become of Galley and Chater.

It was more than six months before the authorities received an anonymous letter giving a hint of the location of Galley's grave. After the body was found another letter from the same writer gave the name of a member of the gang. When this man was captured he turned 'King's Evidence' and seven more were arrested.

The hearing began at Chichester Assizes on 16th January 1749, almost a year after the murders were committed. The prisoners were all found guilty and were sentenced to be executed on the next day. The bodies of five were hung in chains.

After the successful prosecution of the seven, two more were captured and were taken to the assize at East Grinstead where they were convicted and executed. In the same court five more smugglers were sentenced to be hanged for highway robbery and housebreaking. They were taken to Horsham and executed. Two of these men were members of the Hawkhurst Gang who had been spirited out of London's Newgate Prison by smugglers who attacked and overpowered the turnkey.

Five more members of the gang were tried at the Old Bailey on 4th April 1749, on a charge of breaking into the Poole custom house and stealing thirty-seven hundredweights of tea valued at £500. Two of the men were described by the prosecutor as 'reckoned the most audacious wicked fellows amongst the smugglers, and both equally concerned in the long list of atrocities with which the notorious Hawkhurst Gang was credited'. They were Thomas Kingsmill, aged twenty-eight years, and William Fairall, aged twenty-five. Both were sentenced to death.

Next day they were conveyed to Tyburn under strong military guard and were hanged. The bodies were taken down and carried to a smith's shop in Fetter Lane where chains were fitted. Kingsmill's body was hung at Goudhurst Gore and Fairall's at Horsendown Green, near his home.

I have dealt at some length with this notorious gang, but there were others equally villainous working most parts of the coasts of the United Kingdom.

The situation had become so alarming by 1751 that a naval officer proposed to the government that 2,060 officers and men, in sixty ships, should be sent to patrol round the coasts of Great Britain and Ireland to stop the running of goods. The scheme received no support, due mainly to the cost likely to be involved.

However, the Custom Department was given more and better equipment, including fast sailing cutters. Unfortunately the quality of the manpower employed showed no improvement, and the service was the laughing stock of the country. The men were generally inefficient, corrupt and cowardly. They got no co-operation from the Navy whose seamen objected to being placed under their command, as did detachments of dragoons. Men from the armed services were more likely to help than hinder the smugglers, and were known to sell them government stores.

The oldest section of the preventive service was the riding officer force whose job it was to patrol the coasts on horseback.

The force was created by Act of Parliament in 1697 'for the better and more effectual execution of this and other Acts made against the exportation of wool, it be enacted that certain Commissioners (eight-six in all) or any five of them be authorised for putting this and other the said laws into execution and are hereby impowered from time to time, by their agents or substitutes to be deputed . . . to seize all wool and other things mentioned which shall be endeavoured to be transported contrary to this Act'. This was the first provision against export smuggling.

Mr Baker, the Supervisor of Customs for Kent and Sussex noted in his report for 1703 that there were fifty riding officers patrolling 200 miles of coast from the Isle of Sheppey to Emsworth, Hampshire.

The use of soldiers to assist the riding officers continued throughout the eighteen century but red tape, as well as the reluctance of the troops impaired its effectiveness, as can be seen from a directive from the Treasury dated 25th January, 1787, that when officers of the Revenue were in need of military assistance the Board 'should in the first instance apply to the Secretary of War who would, if the service should admit it, afford the assistance required'. This procedure ensured that by the time authority was given the reason for the request had usually passed.

The opinion of one soldier of this duty can be gauged by a letter signed 'old soldier' which appeared in *Monthly Intelligence* for 1737. He deplored the deterioration of the military spirit amongst officers: 'I am sorry to say there are some officers who

26

never desire to make a campaign, except against the smugglers, some who would be much better pleased to watch all night for the seizure of tea and brandy than to march into trenches; and I do assure you they had much rather be commanded by a Custom House officer than Prince Eugene or the Duke of Marlborough'.

The troops shared in the rewards for seizures, but squabbles frequently ensued, and, in February, 1783, directions were issued to collectors and comptrollers to 'retain in their hands so much out of the Custom Officer's shares of seizures as would appear to be due to the soldiers'.

Although employed under the riding officers the army was empowered by an Act of 1805 to seize ships and goods, and to arrest offenders without commissions from the Revenue Boards.

The state of almost complete lawlessness continued until the early years of the nineteenth century, when the threat of a French invasion caused serious alarm to the government and the country. For reasons of national defence a drive started to improve the efficiency of the Customs service and the Preventive Waterguard was established, in 1809.

With the creation of the waterguard the riding officers establishment was reduced to one inspector and 120 riding officers, but by 1821 the staff had increased to six inspectors, at £150-£180 per year with an allowance of £35 for a horse; three temporary inspectors and 120 riding officers at from £65-£90 with £30 for a horse, and twenty-eight temporary riding officers, making a total staff of 157 at a cost of £19,507 17s. 1¼d.

Finally, a further insight of what has been called, perhaps with understandable cynicism, the good old days can be gained from Customs Outport Records for the south coast.

The behaviour of a Riding Officer was the subject of a report on 3rd October 1771: We beg leave to observe that William Phipps, Riding Officer at Newtown, upon incidents is very capable of his duty but greatly addicted to drinking. He promised us last Christmas that he would leave off, but we find he has not, and we think it is greatly owing to his living in a public house and, tho' we have advised him to remove from thence, he says he cannot because there are but few houses in the place, and he cannot get a lodging at any of them, but where he is.

18th June 1772: In obedience to your commands of the 2nd December last, we reprimanded William Phipps, Riding Officer of this Port and enjoined him to more temperance in future, and acquainted him that he must immediately provide himself with another lodging, which he has accordingly done, and he has we have been assured by the Supervisor behaved very well ever since.

Customs have always had the right to seize the vehicle used to transport contraband but this can provide problems as the next two entries show:

6th February 1779: In return to your order of the 26th ult. We beg leave to report that the boat therein mentioned is not fit to be employed or used in the service. She is $43\frac{1}{2}$ feet in length and in breadth $7\frac{1}{2}$ feet, rows with fourteen oars and carries four masts, and was evidently built for the purpose of smuggling only, and will if sold no doubt be bought to be used again in that trade. We submit whether it will not be best to have her cut up and sold as firewood.

12th August 1780: Annexed we transmit an account of a seizure of eleven gallons of foreign brandy together with a horse, bridle and saddle, seized by Stephen Squire, an officer of this Port. As the expense of keeping the horse, if not soon condemned and sold, will exceed the value of it, we pray your Honours' orders for prosecuting the same before the Justices.

A complaint that the smugglers were becoming too daring because of the leniency of the law is contained in another entry dated 16th April 1781: That smugglers in general are become more daring than ever, more frequently assemble in numbers carrying arms and in disguise, and that instances very often occur of officers being wounded, beaten, opposed and obstructed, is a fact which I fear your Honours are but too well acquainted with. I humbly apprehend this is in some measure owing to the lenity of the Legislature who in passing the Act of the 19th of His present Majestie, Chapter 69, have only subjected persons convicted of obstructing officers or rescuing goods after seizure, to the punishment of the House of Correction, or to serve His Majestie by sea and land for a limited time, which there is reason to believe has frequently proved an encouragement to smugglers and ill-disposed persons to obstruct, oppose and illtreat Officers of the Revenue, rather than a means of deterring them from such atrocious offences.

An example of the lenience complained of was recorded on

24th January 1782: William Wall, who in our letter of the 11th inst. we acquainted your Honours had been committed to the County Gaol for obstructing Stephen Squire, one of the officers of this port in the execution of his duty, was tried for this offence at the Quarter Sessions held at Winchester on the 17th inst. and being convicted thereof was sentenced to suffer eighteen month's imprisonment, and to be kept during this time at hard labour, he not appearing to be a fit person to serve His Majestie either in the sea or land service.

A sentence unlikely to have been a serious deterrent to the bloodthirsty villains who guarded the smuggling gangs in the bad old days.

2
The Coast Blockade

Records at the end of the eighteenth century show the size of the smuggling problem which faced the government.

In 1779 the greater part of the 3,867,000 gallons of gin distilled annually at Schiedam, Holland was earmarked for the English black market. At the same time another distillery was in operation at Dunkirk and its entire output was available to smugglers. The French imported six million pounds of tea, all of it destined for clandestine landing on the south coast.

The Channel Islands were major resorts of the freetraders, and in 1800 the government sent a Mr Stiles to Guernsey as a Commissioner with instructions to stamp out smuggling. His arrival caused consternation, especially when he declared: smuggling from the islands of Guernsey and Aldernay having increased to a great and alarming extent, and the offenders having in some instances committed murder on the revenue officers on the coast of England, the government has it in contemplation to put a stop to such growing and serious evils so highly prejudicial to His Majesty's revenue.

The good people of Guernsey were determined to prevent such a catastrophe and drew up a petition giving a somewhat altruistic account of freetrading. 'They cannot but feel alarm at the proposed plan which is pregnant with ruin to thousands of industrious inhabitants who have carried on the respective trades without interference . . . The wealth gained here reverts to the mother country and helps to support the public funds, promotes the navigation of the country, and, in time of war the means of fitting out numerous privateers to the great annoyance of the enemy's trade . . . That the suppression of the trade of this island would be productive at all times of the most fatal consequences to the inhabitants, would annihilate large capitals and eliminate the property of every man in the island to one-half of its value, and

30

reduce thousands of innocent and industrious persons to beggary and ruin'.

At this time the Royal Courts of Guernsey reported: There is no doubt from ten to twelve thousand guineas are every week carried by smugglers to the continent.

The freetraders bought their goods for cash or with English wool which they illicitly exported to France.

The lawlessness on the coasts was matched in the capital itself, and London was a dangerous place for the guardians of law and order.

It was two o'clock in the morning when the watchmen of St Pauls, Covent Garden and St Martins-in-the-Fields seized 100 hundredweights of tea, together with three men, a boy and a string of pack-horses. Five other members of the gang escaped after drawing their cutlasses and threatening the watch.

A few days later, two women walking in a city street, large baskets balanced on their heads, were stopped and searched. The baskets contained 117 pounds of tea. The sobbing prisoners were marched to the watch-house where they broke down and confessed that they worked for smugglers. To show that they repented they offered to lead their captors to a house where tea was stored.

The officer in charge of the watch sent the women to the house escorted by four of his men, but, as they walked down Bunhill Row, the women screamed 'robbers, robbers', and at the signal the smugglers galloped out of an alley, battered the watchmen to death with their whipstocks, and escaped with the women.

The government was alarmed, and Parliament authorized the setting up of the Preventive Waterguard, in 1809.

The waterguard was to supplement the work of the revenue cruisers and riding officers, and was under the direction of the Board of Customs, with the revenue cruisers included in its establishment.

The coasts of England were divided into three districts. The first with twenty-three cruisers and forty-two preventive boats covered the area from London to Land's End; the second with ten cruisers and thirteen preventive boats from Land's End to Carlisle, and the third from London to Berwick had nine cruisers and thirteen preventive boats. Naval captains were appointed Inspecting Captains and were issued with tenders in which they were to sail up and down the coasts of their district, checking that the ships under their command were carrying out their allotted duties.

The men of the waterguard were offered rewards for the capture of smugglers and contraband, but, although the organization was increased in size and its equipment was improved during the following seven years, it achieved only limited success.

A Treasury minute dated 2nd February, 1816, records the transfer of the cruisers to the Admiralty and the Preventive Waterguard to the Treasury 'that a great and most useful improvement may be made in the establishment of preventive boats on many parts of the coast by increasing their numbers . . . by boats looking out whenever it is safe for a boat to keep the sea, so as to be a guard along shore from station to station, and it has been represented to their Lordships that the smugglers avail themselves of opportunities to run across the Channel and land their cargoes when the cruisers are compelled by stress of weather to seek shelter in ports and roads, at which times the crews of these boats, from the information it will be their duty to acquire, may be eminently useful in watching the possible landing places in their neighbourhood'.

This minute indicates that although intended primarily for patrol work at sea, the waterguard was also expected to patrol on shore in bad weather.

Under the new direction the waterguard appears to have been regarded as reasonably efficient, and, in 1821 was established in Scotland under a Captain-General, with 146 men divided between nineteen stations, but only limited stretches of the coast were supervised – Berwick to North Berwick, and, Katerline, Kincardineshire to Buckie in Banffshire.

Ireland's waterguard had been set up two years earlier, as an experiment, on the coast of Cork. The following year it was extended from Waterford to the Giant's Causeway at Ballycastle, County Clare, and on the coast of Kerry from St John's Point in Donegal Bay to Lough Swilly.

The Instructions issued to the force described its object as: to prevent the landing of smuggled goods, whereby the arrangements made by the smugglers on shore may be defeated; the disposal of tobacco, if ultimately landed, rendered difficult

'Saved' drawn by J. D. Watson, 1866, from a picture in the Watch-house of South Shields Volunteer Life Brigade (See chapter six)

The New Romney lifeboat was launched in a blizzard in 1891 to assist two schooners wrecked at Littlestone. Three Coastguard volunteers in the crew were lost with four victims from the wrecks. All were buried with ceremonial honours (See chapter seven)

Coastguards at pistol firing
practice (See chapter eight)

Portable searchlight used by
Coastguards for cliff searches
(See chapter thirteen)

and dangerous, and the probability of capturing the vessels, crews and cargoes by the Revenue Cruisers or His Majesty's Ships materially increased.

Each station was equipped with two boats and a supply of arms and ammunition.

The duties and organization of each district were also laid down in a Treasury minute of 1821. Each was under an Inspecting Commander, an ex-naval revenue cruiser captain, who was invested with full command over the Chief Officers, boats and crews, and was responsible for discipline, good conduct and obedience to instructions of his men.

The commander was required to visit each station in his district as often as practicable, both by day and by night; to inspect journals, watch-houses, boathouses, arms and ammunition, boats and stores; to exercise the chief officers and crews frequently in the use of arms, in order that they could protect themselves, and, in the use of life-saving apparatus. This is the first mention of life-saving duties which were to become, after the first world war, the main reason for the continued existence of the Coastguard.

The commander was required to perform his journeys on horseback, and to proceed as much as possible by the sea coast. He was also to keep up communication with the commanders of vessels of war, and, revenue cruisers, and with other persons employed in the vicinity in the protection of the revenue, in order that concerted action might be taken against smugglers.

Each station which had a crew of eight or more was supplied with a six-oared galley and a four-oared gig, and stations with six or less with a four-oared gig. A 'wall-piece' – a long musket on a swivel, muskets or carbines, pistols, bayonets and cutlasses, with the necessary ammunition were supplied to each station.

Chief officers were in charge of the stations and were required to search and strictly rummage all suspicious ships, vessels or boats coming within the limits of their stations, and to seize all prohibited goods together with the ships, vessels or boats if liable to seizure. They were also directed to exercise their own judgement as to going to sea or on land patrols, taking care to keep their boats always ready to go afloat. They were to visit all creeks and bye-places within the limits of their guard by boat as often as wind, weather and other circumstances permitted.

B

The crews were composed of Commissioned Boatmen and Boatmen. They were required to be out either afloat or patrolling the coast at least five nights a week, and were ordered to confine their duties to the sea coast and on no account to go any distance inland in pursuit of smugglers.

No member of the service was allowed to serve on a station within twenty miles of his birthplace or home, and he was required to live as near to his station as possible. Where accommodation was provided the men were required to pay rent, unless they lived in watch-houses or on vessels used as such.

Any officer intermarrying with the family of a reputed smuggler or lodging in his house, or 'contracting any improper intimacy with him' was liable to be dismissed.

It was impressed on all officers that their first and most important duty was to secure the person of the smuggler, and to encourage them to do so they were awarded twenty pounds for a capture. The arrested smugglers were usually impressed – pressganged into the navy.

Other duties performed by the waterguard included the enforcement of quarantine regulations and receivership of wrecks.

In spite of the improvements in equipment, discipline and manpower the waterguard was not the scourge of the smugglers that had been intended, and the time had come for a complete reappraisal of the preventive set-up.

Four years earlier, old Jock McCullough, a tough Scottish naval captain had realized that the preventive system was a farce. It was his vision and foresight which produced a plan which would satisfy the needs of the moment, and at the same time solve a major problem for the Admiralty.

With the ending of the Napoleonic wars, Parliament was no longer to be persuaded to vote the cash required to keep even, what the navy considered, a minimum number of ships in commission. Almost the entire Fleet was ordered to be 'mothballed', and the crews turned out to grass with little prospect of civilian employment. If he was lucky the discharged matelot might be given a permit to beg – or perhaps a chance to join a band of smugglers.

The danger of once more leaving the country virtually undefended, and with the bulk of their small budget likely to be swallowed up by the half-pay to which hundreds of officers were entitled, led the Admiralty to back the plan to establish a Naval Protective Guard, which was to become a thorough blockade of the coasts of Kent and Sussex by ships of the Royal Navy.

It was soon realized that the blockade was seriously hampering the smugglers and the Admiralty was delighted, but it was the plan of Jock McCullough, then commanding H.M.S. *Ganymede,* which led to the formation of what was, although without the title, His Majesty's Coastguard.

McCullough drew up an appreciation of the situation and expounded the proposal which he considered would lead to the complete cessation of smuggling. This was a plan to complement the Protective Guard or Coast Blockade as it was known, by hunting the smugglers on land as well as at sea.

The riding officer system had long been in disrepute and the obvious answer, declared McCullough, was for the navy to take over those duties and co-ordinate the drive against the free-traders.

The scheme was accepted with some reservations by the Admiralty. Their Lordships were not prepared to authorize the formation of a land-based force, but would allow the men of the Fleet to be landed at night for shore patrolling, on condition that they were re-embarked by sunrise.

The experiment was an unqualified success and it seemed that at last the smugglers had been put out of business.

The scheme was placed on an official footing on 19th June 1817 when the establishment of the Coast Blockade, an entirely naval concept, was authorized – a date which must be regarded as the unofficial birthday of the Coastguard Service.

The Blockade was first maintained by the men of the frigate H.M.S. *Severn* to which Captain McCullough had been posted. She took station in the Downs, and her crew was landed and established posts in the Martello Towers, which had been built as anti-invasion forts between the North and South Foreland when Napoleon threatened a landing.

Where no towers were available barrack-type buildings were erected to accommodate the men, and many of these 'blockade stations', renovated from time to time, were still in use as Coast-guard Stations at the beginning of the twentieth century. They were fitted out in naval fashion, the men slept in hammocks and lived in 'long-rooms'. Married quarters were a corner of the long-room screened off with sail canvas.

With the arrival of the Navy, the boats and men of the Preventive Waterguard, who had been stationed between the Forelands were withdrawn.

The Blockade was later extended from North Foreland to the Isle of Sheppey on one side, and from South Foreland to Seaford on the other.

As the work of the blockade increased H.M.S. *Severn* was replaced by a famous man-o'-war H.M.S. *Ramillies* which had fought under the command of Sir Thomas Masterman Hardy in the American war. H.M.S. *Hyperion* was stationed at Newhaven.

Discipline was strict and the work was unpopular among the sailors. Men who committed minor offences were sent to *Ramillies* to be 'dusted down' as a flogging was called by the crew. It was claimed that the better class of seamen would not join the service, and that those who did connived with the smugglers, got drunk or deserted. The most general complaint was that the quartermasters had too much power and were brutal to the men under their command.

The blockade stations were under command of Lieutenants of the Royal Navy. Each station comprised a number of watchtowers, each in charge of a petty officer with the rating of Quartermaster.

Nevertheless, in spite of all the criticism from within the service, the Admiralty considered the scheme a success, and a year after its inception, the blockade was extended to cover the coast from Sheerness to Seaford, and later to most of the coasts where smuggling was rife.

At the same time the Revenue Cutter Service was developed to deal with the more notorious smuggling centres, and the men of this service were detached to form boat crews.

The duty of these crews was to patrol the coast in their boats during the night. To ensure that the work was properly done, the 'sitter' as the officer in charge of the boat was called, was ordered to take soundings at certain times during the night, and to forward these to the Inspecting Commander.

One omission which made much of the work ineffective was a realistic intelligence service to provide information about smugglers' plans and activities. Some of the more energetic officers would have their boats rowed ashore, pulled up above high water mark and camouflaged. The men would then don old clothes and disperse to the local hostelries where they eavesdropped on the talk and gossip in the bars. Any news of a 'run' was reported to the cutter's captain on the following morning.

The next development of importance in the story of the Blockade was the establishment of permanent boat-crews for the 'preventive boats' as they were called. The crews were stationed ashore and this presented its own problem as there was enmity between the preventive men and the local populations. Those who had been vociferous in demanding the curbing of smuggling gangs soon realized that the suppression of freetrading was forcing up the cost of living. No longer could they enjoy the low prices of smuggled luxury goods.

Couch's *History of Polperro* records that: though active opposition was not politic, the people determined to offer as much passive resistance as was safe. None would let a 'blockader' a house to live in at any price, so the whole force was obliged to make a dwelling and guardhouse of the hull of a vessel which was moored to the old quay.

In official documents the force was now described as the Preventive Waterguard, with duties including the rowing of guard in their boats at night, and, patrolling the land when the weather prevented the boat being launched.

The officers of the Waterguard were mainly Lieutenants R.N., but there are records of appointments of Civilian Officers. These were men chosen from the mates and gunners of the Revenue Cruisers who were designated Chief Officer regardless of their previous rank.

Despite all its problems the Coast Blockade was remarkably successful, and a report shows that in one year ninety-six houses in Deal, Kent, were closed for want of tenants, and, the gaols were filled with smugglers. Such success was regarded with little pleasure by the freetraders of the south coast. The blockaders were described by them as 'base tools of a despotic government'. The smugglers were not prepared to submit to what they considered an unwarranted attack on their rights and vested interests. The more violent organized armed gangs to terrorize the blockaders. Deaths were numerous on both sides, but there was no

37

glory to be won in such battles and few records have survived of this first successful attack on smuggling which certainly broke the back of the problem.

One Blockade officer, Lieutenant Charles Brand received an anonymous letter when he was stationed at Eastbourne: 'Sir, you had better not be so harde on us for if you do we will knok out youre branes the furst time we ketch you alone in the dark, and we will kill youre dog'. This was a reference to a Newfoundland dog which was expert at sniffing out smugglers' hiding places, and had led Blockaders to several dumps of contraband.

Lieutenant Brand was lucky and escaped the wrath of the smugglers, but his successor walked into an ambush, in a lonely hedge-lined lane, and fell riddled by bullets. Mortally wounded, he crawled to a nearby house and, with the last of his strength knocked on the door and begged for help. The occupants refused to open the door and left him to expire on the doorstep.

The Coast Blockaders got little support from the magistrates, many of whom were in the pay of the smugglers, or went in fear of reprisals. So many complaints were made against the force that it was deemed necessary to lay down stringent instructions.

Commissioned officers were warned that at no time were they to go on duty without their commissions. Before a search was made for smuggled goods a 'writ of assistance' from the Inspecting Commanders was required. No warehouse, house or shop was to be entered without a writ, and never after sunset. A local constable or law enforcement officer had to accompany the searchers, and, a full report on the operation was required by the Comptroller-General as soon as possible afterwards.

It was strictly forbidden to interfere with the inhabitants of the coastal towns and villages, except in the execution of duty. Nor were the Blockaders to encroach on the manors or interfere with manorial rights, or destroy game or trespass.

Popular or not, the Coast Blockade was extended until it covered the entire seaboard of the British Isles before it was disbanded in 1831.

Before turning to the events which led to the official birth of the Coastguard, mention must be made of the work of the Revenue Cruisers which from the seventeenth century patrolled the coasts against smuggling.

The start of the service can no longer be traced in official documents, but in June 1698 'Instructions to the Captains of Sloops' were approved, and a few months later a Mr Godolphin wrote a paper advocating the patrolling of the coasts of Britain by sloops.

These proposals were accepted, and boats known as Customs House Sloops or smacks set sail, each with a master, mate and crew.

In 1713 regulations were published for the division of rewards. Seizures were to be divided half to the master, a quarter to the mate and the remainder to the crew.

The activities of the cruisers were well regarded, and orders were given in 1724 for the building of a further seven sloops for service off the coast of Scotland.

The duties of the Masters of the Smacks are described in Crouch's *Complete Guide* dated 1732: The Masters of Smacks etc. who are appointed to command vessels to cruise on the coasts of Great Britain are diligently to attend on board, and to keep their vessels in constant motion within their respective Districts or Stations, unless in cases of necessity or pursuit of suspected vessels. And in cruising they are to speak with all ships or vessels which they shall meet at sea; and if they have reason to suspect they have goods on board designed to be smuggled they are diligently to watch their motions and keep them company till they are clear of the coast within their respective district, in order to prevent the fraudulent landing of any such goods. And they are likewise to endeavour to prevent the exportation of such goods as are prohibited to be exported out of this Kingdom, and in case they discover such goods to have been shipped or shipping for foreign parts they are to seize the same with the vessels etc.

For the due navigation of each of these vessels there are likewise appointed a Mate and a sufficient number of Mariners who are under the direction of the said Masters.

And for the victualling of each of these vessels the Commanders are allowed ninepence a day for themselves and each mariner, whereof notice is to be affixed on the mast that if good and sufficient provisions are not provided by the Commanders, the mariners may complain to the Collector or Comptroller.

These Masters and their Mates are to keep Journals of their daily transactions and proceedings with their motions from place to place; to be delivered monthly to the Collectors of their respective ports in order to be transmitted to the Commissioners.

And by way of distinction all Smacks, Yachts or Vessels employed in the service of the Customs are to wear a Jack and Ensign with the seal of office thereon, the mark in the Ensign being twice as large as that in the Jack; but not to wear a pendant.

Although primarily employed in the protection of the Revenue, these vessels were mobilized from time to time, presumably for coast defence. On the outbreak of war with Spain in 1745 they were placed under the direction of the Admiralty, and the crews were increased. Again in 1779 directions were received from the Treasury: that the several Custom House Vessels be manned and armed to the fullest extent and that they repair to the Downs, Portsmouth and Plymouth to be under the direction of the Commanding Officers there.

The vessels returned to their ordinary duties in the following December. A similar mobilization took place in September 1781 and lasted until October 1782.

Some of the vessels carried formidable armament and were capable of performing useful service if called upon in time of war.

In 1780, commanders of cruisers were permitted to provide themselves with Letters of Marque, at their own expense, during the hostilities, but were informed that the Board would not consent to bear any part of the expense for the repair of damage that might be sustained, where no seizures were made.

The list of cruisers in the service of the Customs in 1784 shows forty-four vessels with crews numbering 1,041 men. The cost of running the fleet was £44,355 16s. 11d, per annum.

The cruisers continued in the Customs service until 1816 when a Treasury Minute, dated February 2nd, transferred control to the Admiralty. The reasons for the transfer were 'the declaration of peace had, by opening up the parts of Europe, restored to the smugglers the advantages they had formerly possessed . . . It appears therefore to be their Lordships' urgent duty to consider by what means it will be practicable to stop the progress of this increasing evil. In this consideration it occurs forcibly to their Lordships' remembrance that after so long a period of war in every part of Europe, many of the most daring professional men, discharged from their occupation, and averse to the daily labour of agricultural or mechanical employment, will be the ready instruments of those desperate persons who have a little capital, and are hardy enough to engage in this traffic.

'The only effectual mode of putting an end to smuggling on the part both of such principals, and agents, is to render this traffic so unprofitable as to discourage persons from carrying it on. This purpose would be most completely accomplished by the diminution of the Import Duties to an extent that should take away the incitement to evade them; this is, however, utterly impracticable, and inconsistent with every view that can now be taken of the necessities and welfare of the country.

'The only mode, therefore remaining, is to increase the danger and hazard to the greatest possible extent to those who are bold enough to engage in it, either as principals or agents, by impressing in every capture the men employed in the vessels and boats (pressganging), and by levying the legal penalties upon those who embark their capital in this nefarious traffic.

'My Lords are of opinion that it will be necessary to establish such a system of discipline and vigilance over the Revenue Cruisers and Boats as shall give to the country the benefit of their constant and active services on the stations assigned them; and that it would add greatly to the efficacy of their exertions if they were put under naval watchfulness and discipline, controlled by such authority as the Department of Admiralty may think fit . . . my Lords are of opinion it will be expedient to concert with the Board of Admiralty for the immediate transfer of the Revenue Cruisers in England and Scotland to their direction'.

The transfer took place on April 15th 1816, and the revenue cruisers remained under the direction of the Admiralty until 1822, the cost being borne by the Customs revenue.

In 1821 the Commissioner of Inquiry expressed the opinion that efficacy of these vessels in protecting the revenue was by no means proportionate to the expense of maintaining them, and recommended that the number be greatly reduced. He also suggested that they should be returned to the control of the Customs, but with the officers and crews selected by the Admiralty. To this the Treasury agreed.

The men of the revenue cruisers had a hard and arduous life.

B*

The vessels were seldom allowed into harbour, except for repairs or to seek shelter in severe storms.

The routine was for the cruisers to move close to land at dusk each day. The boats were lowered and half the crew took to them. They then rowed patrol throughout the night along the coast. They were picked up by the cruiser at a pre-arranged rendezvous. If foul weather blew up, the boat crews could try to find the cruiser or row to shelter.

One old cruiserman told how he was often dropped at one side of the Isle of Wight at night, and picked up on the other side at dawn.

Conditions in winter were appalling, and the only reason for the men's devotion to duty was the chance of a fat reward for spotting a valuable prize.

Even in harbour there was little rest for the crews. As soon as the anchor was dropped, orders were sent on board for the night boat patrols. If the cruiser was in for repairs the crew was landed and marched off to land stations, in areas where smuggling was most rife.

The cruisers were to join the other anti-smuggling services, under control of Customs, following the publication of what was known as the Consolidation Order of the Treasury.

3
Birth of the Coastguard

In 1822 orders were issued by the Treasury that 'the whole of the forces for the prevention of smuggling, consisting of the Revenue Cruisers, Preventive Waterguard, and the Riding Officers, shall be consolidated and be placed under the direction of the Board of Customs'.

This was a major step forward, and for the first time brought the three services under one control, but no mention was made of the Coast Blockade. The Blockade was certainly a 'force for the prevention of smuggling', and the terms of the Consolidation Order make it clear, therefore, that the Blockaders were regarded merely as being on detachment from the Royal Navy.

It was during this re-organization that a suggestion was made that the consolidated force should be called 'The Coastguard', and the title was taken into use on 15th January 1822 in official documents and became the official birthday of the Service.

The Blockade was broken up in March 1831, and as the men of the Navy withdrew they were replaced by personnel from the Revenue Cruisers, and, civilians who were recruited.

There was now a triple cordon guarding the coasts against smuggling – the Revenue Cruisers, the Coastguard and the Mounted Guard.

The Coastguard had developed from detached boat-crews of the Blockade into a disciplined and organized regular force, the men of which, although not officially responsible until much later, soon gained a reputation for heroism in life-saving from wrecks.

On the coast of Fife a Lieutenant Randall rescued more than thirty people during his four years' service at the Coastguard Station.

The chain of command of the Force was headed by the Comptroller-General and Deputy Comptroller-General, both Royal Navy commanders, who had headquarters at 'Coastguard Office, Customs House, London.' Then followed the Inspecting Commander of each district who was in command of a group of coast-guard stations. Each station was controlled by a Chief Officer who had a staff consisting of Chief Boatman-in-Charge, Commissioned Boatmen and Boatmen.

The work of the stations, like that of the revenue cruisers was hard, and it was only the possibility of reward for seizures that kept the men going. As the smuggler was a night owl, the coastguards also worked at night.

Lieutenant the Hon Henry Shore, R.N. who later became Lord Teignmouth, recorded in 1892 a conversation with an old coastguardsman. 'Why Sir, in the winter months we had to be on our guards by dusk, which meant leaving home at four or four-thirty and we never got back again till nearly eight the next morning. The only nights-in we got was when our turn came round to be day watchman at the station – once in ten days or so, and perhaps two nights before the full moon and two nights afterwards, though even then we seldom got more than a half night off if smuggling boats were expected off the coast, and, of course, all the crew had to be out.

'I've often been that done up that I could scarcely walk home, and many is the time I've gone down to the water and washed my face to keep my eyes open. Oh, it was enough to kill a horse I can tell you, only a strong man could stand the work'.

Smugglers rarely ran their goods on moonlight nights, and unless information was received that contraband was to be landed, half the crew of the coastguard station was allowed to rest during the five nights of the full moon.

The daily duty parade was called in the watchhouse at dusk when the entire crew assembled, armed and ready for the night's work. Each man was detailed for guard duty and left for his post under strict orders to speak to no one.

The regulations forbade any communication between the men and their families after they received their orders, and explicitly laid down that no man was to be on guard at the same place for two nights in succession.

The guards were changed at least once during the night to maintain alertness, and the Chief Officer made surprise checks twice nightly.

All this was essential to prevent collusion and to foil the smugglers' spies who would watch the station routine. They were unceasing in their attempts to suborn the coastguardsmen.

Each patrol carried two heavy pistols, several rounds of ammunition, a cutlass and a blue light for raising the alarm.

Sixteen hours a day, in all weather, with ever present danger of being shot, tossed over a cliff or of being kidnapped by smugglers and dumped on the coast of France, required greater rewards than pay and housing. This led to the introduction of prize money, or to use the official description 'Rewards for Seizure', a fixed scale of reward approved for the crews of the revenue cutters and the men of the Coastguard.

The revenue cutters' shareout was:

Commander	100 shares
Chief Mate	45 shares
Second Mate	35 shares
Deputed Mariners	20 shares
Mariners	10 shares
Boys	5 shares

The coastguard stations' shareout was:

Chief Officer	25 shares
Chief Boatman	10 shares
Riding Officer	10 shares
Commissioned Boatmen	8 shares
Boatmen and extra men	6 shares

The prize-money could be one thousand pounds for a single seizure, which when divided between the Chief Officer and the crew of a station could amount to £90 for each boatman.

One safeguard against collusion between coastguards and smugglers was the regulation that 'every man employed in the Waterguard is to make it his first and most material object to secure the person of the smuggler . . . and unless Inspecting Commanders certify that the most active exertions were made to take the smugglers no reward for or share of any seizure whatever will be paid or allowed'.

To encourage the most material object twenty pounds was paid for every smuggler taken and convicted, in addition to the prize-money – a payment described by the smugglers as 'blood money'.

A system of promotion evolved in the coastguard service whereby Chief Boatmen could become Chief Officers, and, by 1862 every coastguard station was in charge of a man promoted from the ranks.

The pay of the coastguards at this time was:

Comptroller-General	£1,000
Deputy Comptroller-General	£500
Inspectors	£800
Assistant Inspectors	£400
Inspecting Commanders	
(if a Naval Officer)	6/-d. per day
(if formerly commander of a revenue cruiser)	£200 per annum
with the following allowances:	
For one horse	£60
For an additional horse	£30
For stationery	£5
Subsistence (not exceeding 70 days a quarter)	10/-d. per day

Chief Officers (if civilian)	£15 and 4/- per day
Chief Officers (if naval officers)	4/- per day
Chief Boatman	£10 and 3/- per day
Commissioned Boatmen and Boatmen	£5 and 3/- per day
Mounted Guard	£60-£75 plus £30 for a horse
Cruisers Commanders	£150 plus £3 for stationery per year
Chief Mates	£60-£80
Second Mates	£40-£45
Gunners, Boatswains, Carpenters and Stewards	£2 8s. 0d. per month
Mariners	£2 per month
Boys	£10 per annum

Naval Officers received the equivalent of half-pay in addition to allowances.

To tighten up discipline and improve efficiency the old method of recruiting was replaced in 1829 by regulations that 'no person is to be admitted as a Boatman in the Coastguard Service unless he has served six years at sea or seven years apprenticeship in fishing boats, and, is twenty and under thirty years of age'.

This was emphasized in a letter from the First Lord of the Admiralty to Earl Grey suggesting improvements to the system of Coast Guard, 'My Lords also entirely agree in the opinion of the First Lord that an appointment in the Coast Guard Service should in every case be held out as a reward for merit and for zeal displayed in H.M. Naval Service'. The letter was the first move in a plan to make the service an adjunct of the Navy, but more of that later.

The system of rowing guards in the Waterguard was gradually dropped, and there was an increase in land patrolling as this was found to be the best method of thwarting the freetraders. However, District Commanders were allowed some freedom of action to take into account the nature of the coastline and the local smuggling habits. On heavily indented coasts the coastguard boats could often sneak up on the smugglers when they were landing contraband in small coves which were inaccessible to the land-based patrols.

The regulations left no doubt about the responsibilities of District Commanders who were 'distinctly to understand that they were held responsible for any smuggling transactions which took place within the limits of their guards'.

Their subordinates were also warned 'The Comptroller-General directs that officers and men be publicly informed that a list will in future be kept of every person serving at a station within which a run took place and that no such officer or man will be considered eligible for promotion or entitled to any mark of indulgence or favour'.

Records of the Cornish coastguard show that this was no slight threat. All promotion was stopped in the Fowey division after a number of smuggling runs.

With the break-up of the Coast Blockade in 1831 another major change took place which converted the Coastguard Service into a naval force, as had been hinted at in the letter to Earl Grey.

The First Lord of the Admiralty, Sir James Graham wrote a letter to the Treasury in March of 1831 drawing attention to the desirability of rendering the Coastguard essentially Naval in all its branches.

'My reason for entertaining this opinion is that great advantage would accrue to the Service from the employment in it of persons who from habit and long experience are better calculated to increase its efficiency than civilians, and because I conceive that the Coastguard Service composed of naval men may be rendered available for great national objects independent of the benefit it will confer by the protection of the Revenue.

'I would remind your Lordships that the employment of naval officers is a direct saving to the country of half-pay which is a part of the remuneration which it is thought equitable to grant for the service of Superior Officers of the Coastguard, and which were civilians employed must be paid over and above the regular allowance.

'The first suggestion which I would make is that instead of the nomination of the Officers and Boatmen of the Coastguard of Scotland and Ireland, and the Boatmen of England resting as at present with the Lords of the Treasury the whole of the Officers and Boatmen be henceforth selected by the Lords of the Admiralty.

' I conceive it to be of essential importance in a service wherein unity of purpose, rapidity of communication and prompt obedience are so eminently requisite that there should be but one directing and controlling power which at the same time should be the source of all promotion and rewards.

'By the adoption of this system I think the Revenue would be more surely protected and in the event of war this guard round the coast of England, composed as it would be of trustworthy naval officers and seamen would perhaps with the addition of a few small armed steam vessels more effectively protect the whole line of coast against any hostile disembarkation than by any other system.

'Another very material and most important advantage which would be consequent on the adoption of this system is the extreme facility it will afford to the collection of seamen for H.M. Navy either by voluntary entry or by impressment, though I am happy in anticipating that the latter mode need less frequently be resorted to when the real benefits and solid advantages of the King's service shall be evidently shown in the Service of the Coastguard composed as I now recommend'.

A Treasury minute dated May 10th 1831, shows that Sir

James' proposals were accepted .'My Lords concur with the First Lord of the Admiralty in the expediency of remodelling the system of the Coastguard Service in Great Britain and Ireland, more especially as regards the appointments and promotions of officers and boatmen, and in the opinion expressed by Sir Jas Graham that in order to increase its efficiency it may be desirable to render it in all its branches essentially naval'.

As a result a nice piece of patronage was transferred to the Admiralty which became responsible for the appointment of officers and boatmen, and entry into the service was then restricted to men from the ships of the Royal Navy or the crews of the revenue cruisers, with encouragement to coastguards' sons to join the cruiser service.

The Regulations approved by the Admiralty on 13th June 1831 for the admission of seamen into the Coastguard may with advantage be reproduced:

1. Vacancies for Boatmen will be filled by seamen as Ships of War are paid off, chosen by their Captain.

2. The Captain shall make this selection with the strictest impartiality and shall certify the men as being the best entitled of the ship's company.

3. Seamen from the Revenue Cruisers may occasionally be admitted.

4. Pay:

Chief Boatman	£10 per annum
Commissioned Boatman and Boatman	£5 per annum

Scale of seizure awards:

Chief Officer	25 shares
Chief Boatman	10 shares
Riding Officer	10 shares
Commissioned Boatman	8 shares
Boatman and extra men	6 shares

In 1832 the reorganization of the Mounted Guard took place,

the main feature of this was the recruitment of volunteers from the Cavalry Regiments and under this system the Riding Officers disappeared.

The coastguard takeover from the Coast Blockade was a simple operation in which the coastguards moved into the watch-houses and buildings, taking over the guard duties with no break in the system.

The officers who had been in command of the blockade stations transferred to the coastguard and remained at their posts, but came under command of the Inspecting Commanders.

The pay scale for the Mounted Guard was issued:

> Superintendent of the Mounted Guard, 6/- per day with £3 per annum for stationery: 5/- to 7/- per day on inspecting duties depending on distance from his residence; 2/- per night for sleeping out; forage for two horses provided by the Crown.
> 12 Sergeants at 5/- per day.
> 24 Corporals at 4/6 per day.
> 124 Privates at 4/- per day.

This made a total force of 161. The men were allowed £25 for the purchase of a horse; £25 for saddlery, and their arms were provided by the Crown.

The cost of the Coastguard Service was shown in a return to Parliament in August 1833. For the year 1832 the cost was:

> Coastguard   £382,491 19s. 6¾d.
> Revenue Cruisers   £145,895 9s. 7¾d.
>   a total of £528,387 9s. 2½d.

The return also showed that there were two Captains and fifty Commanders, R.N. in the Coastguard but no naval captains or commanders in the revenue cruisers.

The *Sussex Advertiser* reported on 4th April 1831 that 'The Coastguard establishment has commenced its duties within the last fortnight and on Thursday twelve horse police (the mounted guard) arrived at Hastings for the performance of the interior duty for the prevention of smuggling. They are rather well-looking men and accoutred in a manner calculated for the service'.

Within two years the Coastguard records were showing successes by the Cornwall men.

July: Forty-two tubs of the Dove's cargo are taken by the boats of the Harpy revenue cruiser and Cawsand and Yealms Stations. Twenty-one tubs are taken by the Cawsand crew in the galley John of Cawsand, the remainder are still sunk off the Eddystone. They are part of a 'crop' belonging to John A—— of Downderry who was seen near Craft Hole lying by a hedge drunk (to avoid losing their goods to the coastguard the smugglers would sink them in tubs attached to anchor chains, until the coast was clear and they could recover them. These strings of sunken tubs were known as crops.)

August: One hundred and fifteen tubs belonging to the Dove were taken by the Looe coastguard. Fifty-seven tubs out of sixty forming the cargo of the Dove are 'crept up' off Downderry by the Looe boat.

(When the coastguards suspected a crop had been sunk they launched two boats with a heavy rope or chain suspended between them and crept (rowed) slowly up and down the area until their trawl tangled with the crop.)

The coastguards were certainly the scourge of the freetraders, but discipline continued to be unsatisfactory in the early years of the service. Bad habits inherited from the coast blockaders, collusion and drunkenness were the most common offences. From August to February 1829 two hundred and fifteen men were dismissed the service, but a large proportion were from the revenue cruisers for mutinous and outrageous conduct.

It can readily be understood that drunkenness was a major problem facing the commanders of the service, with so much free spirits there for the taking. It was regarded as a perk to reserve one or two tubs from a seizure for the refreshment of the crew, or as it was described in a report 'to afford cheerfulness and buoyance of spirits'.

To restore a more sober atmosphere to the service this practice was stamped out and discipline improved.

In 1827 the Chief Officer of the Langston harbour station was charged with allowing a flagon of spirits to be broached by his crew and ordering his men to take the flagon to his home. This drinking episode had resulted in the death of a crewman from excessive alcohol.

Collusion was also rife on the south coast. There had of course been many cases during the blockade, but the advent of the coast-guard produced a serious increase in the problem. Records show that in 1831 two of the mounted guard, two Chief Boatmen and two Boatmen were dismissed from the Deal station, and two years later, a Boatman at the Walmer station was removed for taking a £20 bribe from a smuggler and arranging for a run to take place during his guard.

Bribery was the most common weapon used by the freetraders and instructions were circulated to the Chief Officers of stations giving advice on ways of preventing collusion. They were directed to 'try and discover a bribed man amongst the crew which can with ease be effected by looking to the mode of living of the men and by ascertaining if the men off-watch are really in their beds, as a case lately came to knowledge where a bribed character (a Deal boatman) actually assisted the smugglers in working a cargo of fifty tubs upon the guard of one of his messmates after he had been relieved from daywatch, and of course supposed to be in bed, for which he received a bribe of ten pounds, and returned to his quarters ready for midnight relief'.

It was not always money that was offered and another tempta-tion for the unwary coastguard can be imagined from the order, in the Brighton district in 1831 'There being reason to fear that an attempt will be made to corrupt our men through the medium of females, it is my direction that patrols hold no communication with any person either male or female'.

Some instances show that it was not only the crew that forgot their allegiance. In 1827 Lieutenant B——, R.N. was dismissed for allowing a run to take place with every appearance of conni-vance on his part; for not reporting the run and denying such a landing had taken place; for not attempting to secure the goods after they had been landed; for having withdrawn a patrol from the place where the run occurred and sending him to another guard, and, for having been frequently at the house of and in company with a reputed smuggler.

The officer who succeeded Lieutenan B—— so exasperated

the smugglers by the keenness with which he and his crew pursued them that they slit his throat and threw his body off a cliff.

Lieutenant P——, R.N. Chief Officer at Paignton, Devon, was dismissed for releasing two smugglers who had been arrested while escorting a cart containing contraband; for prevailing upon his crew to sign a false seizure report, and, for concealing the fact that any men were present when a seizure was made of a cart, two horses and forty-six tubs of spirits.

In Norfolk, Lieutenant J——, R.N. was dismissed for continuing an intimacy with a notorious smuggler after having been repeatedly cautioned by his Inspecting Commander.

In a very short time three Chief Officers in succession were dismissed from the Looe, Cornwall station for collusion.

In 1822 the Chief Officer and the Riding Officer at Cromer station in Norfolk were dismissed for allowing themselves to be secured by smugglers.

At Morston, Cromer in 1830, the Chief Officer Thomas C—— was recorded in the General Order Book as: having been tried by a Court of Inquiry for negligence, want of exertion and determination, by which the persons and goods of certain smugglers escaped capture, and being highly blameable in going into a crowd of them without having his cutlass drawn or his pistols ready and by collaring a smuggler and immediately discharging his only pistol thereby leaving himself defenceless and consequently easily secured by the smugglers, also having varied in the accounts he gave of the transaction has been reduced to the rank of Boatman and moved to another station'.

With the establishment of the coastguard, the difficulties connected with planning for a run of goods increased each year. The smugglers realized the importance of abducting patrols as a preliminary to be essential, and the patrols had ever to be on guard.

In the Deal district the Inspecting Commander ordered Chief Officers to 'caution the men against surprise by not allowing anyone to approach their guard till satisfied it is their officer, as I am persuaded the smugglers will attempt to seize them at their posts by assuming a false character. Chief Officers are also to be properly armed and on their guard when passing through plantations, turning corners or near cliff edges as I am informed on

53

the very best authority that each company of smugglers will be accompanied by a number of batmen (local term for the coshes they carried) whose first and grand object will be to secure the officer.

Folkestone district coastguard records show that on the night of 2nd October 1842 a patrol was seized by smugglers at Sandgate and had his weapons taken from him. This was done by whistling to the man who, on going to see who was there, was tripped up by five men who held him down and tried to stifle his cries by choking him. However another patrol heard the shouts and went to his rescue. The smugglers ran off taking the arms with them.

As the smugglers became more desperate, forced runs were a common occurrence on the beaches of the south coast in the first quarter of the nineteenth century. It was in fact the rule whenever a large and valuable cargo was at stake. The smugglers' arrangements were elaborate and included the employment of an armed party or 'fighting gang' for the protection of the tub carriers.

The gangs were armed with swingles – a flail-like weapon, bats – a local term for long ash truncheons, and guns.

The forcing of runs continued until 1833 when a nightlong battle in November of that year led to the deaths of four smugglers and the loss of the entire contraband cargo.

Mr Majendie reporting, in 1833, on the 'disturbed districts of East Sussex to Her Majesty's Commissioners as to the administration and operation of the Poor Law' gave an authoritative description of the smugglers' organization, 'The smugglers are divided into two classes. The carriers or bearers, who receive from five shillings per night and upwards, according to the number of tubs they secure, and batmen, who consider themselves of a superior class.

'They go out in disguise, frequently with their faces blackened, and now with firearms; they confine their services to the protection of others and are paid twenty shillings or more per night, and many, perhaps most of them are at the same time in receipt of parish relief'.

Smugglers were no less violent on the coasts of Scotland, although the trade was less extensive because of the sparseness of the population, but there were freetraders operating in the

Solway Firth in the nineteenth century, and cases are recorded of open defiance of the authorities.

A writer referring to Port William as a noted smuggling centre, quoted a letter dated 18th September 1840 from his friend Mr James McWilliam, formerly Officer of Excise at Wigtown, 'I remember counting two hundred and ten horses laden with tea, spirits and tobacco, accompanied by about half that number of Lingtown men, passing within a mile of the town of Wigtown, in open defiance of the Supervisor, two Excise Officers and about thirty soldiers stationed at Wigtown to assist the revenue officers in the suppression of smuggling.

'About the same time the Supervisor, with about twenty-five soldiers, went to Port William where two luggers were lying ready to discharge their cargoes of contraband goods. One of these luggers mounted twenty-two guns, and the other fourteen, and each had a crew of about fifty men. Upon our arrival on the beach the commander of one of these vessels came on shore and said if the party did not instantly retire he would cause a broadside to be discharge from the ships, and, would land one hundred armed men to clear the beach of us, but, if the party would retire quietly to a distance of three or four miles, so as not to disturb the landing of their goods, he would leave thirty or forty ankers of spirits for us on the beach.

'Our party retired and the captain of the lugger fulfilled his promise by leaving thirty-six casks of spirits for us at the place appointed'. (An anker weighed 112 lbs, and contained eight gallons of spirits.)

It was hardly surprising that collusion was rife amongst the men of the Coast Blockade, and that their bad habits were passed down to their successors, as the army and navy were used as reformatories for captured smugglers.

The law laid down that 'every person found assisting in unshipping any goods may be arrested, and if convicted is to be committed to hard labour in the House of Correction for any term not exceeding three years nor less than one year, but, if any person so convicted is approved of as fit to serve His Majesty, the Justices may adjudge him to serve as a soldier or sailor for the term of five years'.

The result of this was that few ships of the Royal Navy did not have some ex-smugglers amongst their crew.

A final assessment of the values of the Blockade and the Coast-guard of that time is contained in a letter from Mr S. Price Edwards of Customs House, Yarmouth, to William Maclean Esquire, dated 9th March 1839.

'I have not the means at hand to bring more forcibly into view the many defects of the Coast Blockade, but sure am I that the change from that to the Coastguard was one attended by results vastly beneficial to the interest of the Revenue, to say nothing of the superiority of the latter in point of sailorship efficiency over the former.

'The Coast Blockade admitted of more smuggling annually on the shores of the two counties committed to its charge than has occurred in the whole of the United Kingdom in the seven years subsequent to its abolition, and, instead of being a nursery for seamen it was no other than a temporary refuge for the outcasts of Society, one wherein the unequal distribution of Rewards tended materially to facilitate bribery and smuggling, to say nothing of the arbitrary and repugnant laws which governed the proceedings.

'In many of its details it was characterized by a lavish expenditure, but in the executive it was worked under a regime of hungry economy inconsistent with the guardianship of the interest of the Revenue.

'For my part, if I were to throw overboard the good of the public revenue, I should at once say "give me the Coast Blockade in preference to the Coastguard".'

The coastguards had from the beginning done much humanitarian work, saving lives from shipwrecks and salvaging wrecks, but they had never been paid for these extra duties. In 1839 however, Lieutenant Wylde and his crew, stationed on the Northumbrian coast, claimed for salvage services from the owners of the *Lapwing*, and were awarded £60 as salvage.

The Coastguard was now an Admiralty service, and the next step was perhaps obvious. Here was a body of fully trained sailors which could be invaluable to the Royal Navy in time of war.

In a General Memorandum dated 21st January 1839 the Admiralty 'desired' that no more landsmen either for general service or for particular ships were to be entered by the officers of the Coastguard, and, a week later another memorandum instructed officers of the Coastguard engaged in raising men for the Navy only to enter Able Seamen in future unless there was an opportunity of sending men direct by a tender or revenue cruiser to the Flagship for which they were destined.

The stage was set for the development of a new role for the service.

4
Great Gun Exercise

The utilization of the Coastguard as a reserve for the Royal Navy in wartime was a natural development.

With the decline in the volume of smuggling, it was accepted that a large force of trained men in the revenue protection services should be made available for the defence of the country in an emergency.

In 1845 a regulation was introduced requiring seamen joining the Coastguard to sign an agreement to serve on board H.M. Ships if required, and by this regulation the Service became a Royal Naval Reserve.

Three years later two hundred coastguards were sent to man ships for service in Ireland.

But for the change of role the Coastguard might have been disbanded along with other preventive services. It was suggested in Parliament that their cost far exceeded the value of the contraband and vessels seized. The House of Commons was told that between 1822 and 1824 the Coast Blockade, Preventive Waterguard and Riding Officers seized 135,000 gallons of brandy; 227,000 gallons of gin; 596 gallons of wine; 253 gallons of rum; 19,000 lbs. of tea; 42,000 yards of silk and 3,000 lbs. of snuff together with 129 vessels and 746 boats. But the sale of the seizures produced only £2,825,000 – about one-eighth of the cost of running the preventive services; rewards; legal expenses and storage costs.

The administration of the force was based on clear recognition of the dual role and measures were introduced to increase its efficiency as a naval reserve. The men of the Coastguard had been introduced to military drill in 1840, when they were ordered to be ready to protect themselves and, where necessary, to assist the civil power during the Chartist riots.

On 2nd May 1845 came the first memorandum proposing the use of the Coastguard for coast defence. The memorandum explained the value of placing large calibre guns at strategic points on the coast 'not so much for the protection of landing places as in expectation that by this extensive range with shot or shell they may deter the enemies' steam vessels from approaching the coast and afford protection to the coasting trade. Regard must also be had to the situation of the Coastguard Stations and on the force of each, as on them will depend the working of the gun, though it is probable that in the first instance the same together with the ammunition will be placed in charge of a sea-man gunner'.

The order was given for 'one man, young and likely to receive instruction' to be sent from certain coastguard stations to the nearest port for the purpose of being instructed in the great gun exercise.

This experiment was a success, and the Comptroller-General ordered the entire force to be trained in the drill as quickly as possible. Crews including men from the revenue cruisers were sent in relays for a one-week course, until all men under fifty years of age had received instruction.

Two years after the initial experiment the first inspection, by the First Lord of the Admiralty, took place, and the Naval and Military Gazette of 14th August 1847 described the scene.

'On Tuesday morning the Lords of the Admiralty proceeded to Southsea Castle to inspect the progress made by the Coast-guard men under the tuition of Commander Jerningham, in their organization as a defensive coast brigade. Their Lordships were attended by Captain H. Stewart, the Comptroller-General of the Coastguard, Captain Chads of the Excellent, Commander O. Oakes, Inspecting Commander of the District, Lieutenant Pritchard of the Chameleon cutter and other officers.

'The inspection took place in the Marine Battery where ninety-two men were assembled, of these twelve only were men-o'-war's men within the last five years. About thirty only of the whole have served in men-o'-war some fifteen years ago. The remainder were cruisers' men and coastguardmen who had entered the service from cruisers.

'They were drilled very smartly by Commander Jerningham.

'Their Lordships were very pleased with the result of their visit and before leaving the battery, the Earl of Auckland publicly addressed the whole body and said he was highly gratified,

59

and the Lords of the Admiralty were very pleased with what they had seen of the rapid proficiency attained by the brigade'.

Commenting on the inspection in the same issue the gazette pontificated: 'We have read with much satisfaction an account of the inspection of a body of the Coastguard by the First Lord of the Admiralty and Captain Houston Stewart, Comptroller-General of the Coastguard which took place at Southsea on the morning of the 9th inst.

'The force assembled on the occasion consisted of ninety-two men, viz. fifty-three from stations and thirty-nine from cruisers, and the progress made by these men, after the very short period of instruction they have received in the new system of drilling in the exercise of the great gun, as at present practiced in the Navy, must have exceeded the most sanguine expectations of their Lordships.

'Before the expiration of the present year a considerable increase in the numbers of men trained and qualified in the new drill will have taken place, and by next year we have every reason to believe, judging from the rapid proficiency already made, that this force will be constituted a most valuable defensive Coast Brigade, and thus the Coastguard will add further to its already important and valuable qualities to the country'.

The keenness of the men brought a message to the force from the Comptroller-General on 11th February 1850. 'I believe that Her Majesty has not a more respectable body of officers and men in her dominions. I must always recollect with peculiar satisfaction . . . the invariable zeal and cheerful intelligence displayed throughout those districts in which the great gun exercise has been established. Should the time of trial come, I am convinced that Her Majesty may securely rely upon the loyal efforts of the Coastguard to aid in any operations, offensive or defensive which shall be undertaken for the protection of the country. Houston Stewart'.

Records show that a gunnery department of the Coastguard was formed under Commander Jerningham, and the stations were issued with wooden replicas of the guns for training purposes.

It was in the following year that the man who can be regarded as the 'father' of the Coastguard, died.

A General Order dated 13th November 1851 stated: The Board of Customs, and, Comptroller-General of the Coastguard

Service desire to record their sense of the loss which the Coast-guard Service has sustained in the death of Commander Samuel Sparshott, R.N. which took place on the 10th inst. at 10 a.m., and whose long experience and zealous attention to the duties of his office as Deputy Comptroller-General of the Coastguard during a period of nearly twenty-five years the Board of Customs and Comptroller-General have fully appreciated.

On 15th August 1853 an 'Act for the Establishment of a Body of Naval Coast Volunteers, and for the temporary transfer to the Navy in case of need of seafaring men employed in other Public Services' laid down that wherever an emergency shall arise which in the opinion of the Lord High Admiral renders it advisable to require the services in H.M. Navy of all or any of the officers and men of the Coastguard and of H.M. Revenue Cruisers, and seamen-riggers, or any of them to join His Majesty's Navy, those so ordered shall join such of H.M. Ships . . . and shall continue to serve . . . but in no case without their consent for a longer period than five years'.

But it was soon clear that the Naval Coast Volunteers had little public appeal and was completely ineffectual. Three years after the Act Sir Charles Woods stated that the Coast Volunteers had failed to answer the design for which they were called into existence. 'Only seventy-three have actually come into employment for a very few days, and unless they can be placed on a better footing there is no use keeping them up'.

His report showed that the strength on paper was 4,819 men in March 1856 and by the following month it had dropped to 4,700. Of this number 1,500 men were in Scotland where Coastguard Stations were not numerous.

'The volunteers are not much to be relied on' was his verdict on 1,000 enrolled on the south coast, 'most are comparatively young lads to whom the temporary duty of protecting the revenue could not be entrusted, most are both young and inefficient and scarcely fit for the rating of 2nd class ordinary seaman'.

The Act had given authority to raise a number of men, not exceeding ten thousand, from among seafaring men and others who might be deemed suitable, to serve for five years. The Volunteers were to be instructed and exercised in seamanship, gunnery and the use of arms, on shore or on board any ships 'rendering such Volunteers fit to be employed in aiding the regular naval forces'. They could be called out for not more than twenty-eight days each year, and could not be taken beyond fifty leagues from the shore of some part of the United Kingdom.

The Coastguard was issued with a naval-type uniform with a leather hat bearing a crown at the front and a ribbon inscribed with 'Coastguard' round it. Difficulties arose over the officers' uniform as the Royal Navy objected to 'civilian' officers wearing navy epaulettes.

This problem was solved by the issue of a dress order. Naval Officers holding appointment as Inspecting Commanders, Chief Officers of Stations, and, Mates of Cruisers were to wear the greatcoat established by Admiralty regulation, with epaulettes, cap and sidearms. Commanders of Cruisers if not naval officers were to wear a blue Lappel-coat buttoned back with nine Coastguard uniform-buttons and notched button-holes, plain blue stand-up collar with gold lace loop and button on each side thereof, the loop to be five inches long, and the lace three-quarters of an inch in breadth. There were also to be three buttons and notched buttonholes on each cuff and pocket as well as three buttons in the folds of each skirt. The waistcoat was to be white or blue Kerseymere with uniform buttons, white or blue pantaloons or trousers worn with boots. A blue cloth cap similar in shape to those worn in the Royal Navy with two bands of gold lace three-quarters of an inch broad, one at the top and the other at the bottom of the headpiece. The sword was to have a plain lace knot and fringe tassel with a black leather belt. White trousers were to be worn on all inspections and special occasions between 23rd April and 14th October, and blue trousers during the winter.

Recruiting remained a problem and attempts were made to improve facilities for the coastguards. Libraries were set up with 50,000 books available for distribution to the stations, but it was laid down that the books must be of a religious, useful and instructive nature.

As the supply of naval officers prepared to serve in the coast-guard dried up, Mates with five years' service in the Navy or revenue cruisers were appointed Chief Officers of Coastguard Stations. Their pay, in 1851, was 9/- a day. Civilian officers with command of two stations were paid £100 a year but had £9 deducted for the rent of their quarters.

In order to get rid of the older R.N. officers a pension scheme was introduced, in 1849, in which any officer applying to retire had to have at least ten years' service, and to be incapacitated by ill-health or age, and to have served in the Coastguard at the end of May 1849. The pensions were £30 per year.

The men of the service started their own scheme by paying 6d. per month and this gave widows £25 plus a pound for each child.

However the shortage of officers continued and in 1853 men were promoted from the ranks. Long-serving Chief Boatmen were given an extra 1/- a day and were placed in charge of small stations. This boosted morale, and encouraged the men to work for promotion.

The cost of the service continued to run at about half a million pounds.

In 1844 a Select Committee on the Tobacco Trade was told by the Comptroller-General that the total force on shore and afloat numbered 6,167 men. There were 4,886 on shore and 1,281 in the revenue cruisers. The cost was £512,168. The Committee reported on the 'failure of the Customs and Coastguard to prevent smuggling' and considered the quantity of tobacco seized to be small. They advised that reductions in the high duties on tobacco would be the best means of putting down smuggling.

Four years later another Select Committee on the Board of Customs reported that the Coastguard cost £510,391 in 1848. There were seventy cruisers and tenders varying in size from 164 to twenty-five tons, including the *Vulcan,* a steam vessel.

There was a last outbreak of large-scale smuggling in 1850 after which the freetraders, who had challenged and often outwitted the revenue protection services, were put out of business. Not by their opponents but by government action – the reduction of import and customs dues. Smuggling, of course continued in a small way, but there were no more runs of goods on lonely beaches, the old methods faded into local folklore, and the notorious smugglers became legendary heroes.

One curious sidelight on life at coastguard stations at that time is shown in records from Kent where donkeys were provided for carrying stores.

The General Order Book for Folkestone district in January 1839 reports: The Board have expressed disapprobation at the amount hitherto charged for forage for donkeys in this district, adding that in their opinion the purchase of beans is wholly unnecessary and also that too many oats have been given. June 15th 1947: The Board having ordered the disposal of the donkey at twenty-seven tower, I have to direct in the first place that the one now at that station be exchanged for one at Lydd station, as complaints of the latter have been made to me of his being of vicious habits. As soon as this exchange takes place, the commanding boatman at twenty-seven tower will sell the Lydd donkey at Dymchurch by public auction.

As the volume of smuggling decreased, the Coastguard devoted much time to lifesaving, and they were equipped with rockets which could fire a lifeline to a wrecked ship. However the shortage of manpower meant that in some areas large sections of the coast were not adequately patrolled, and the loss of life in shipwrecks was enormous. This was a period when there was a huge coastal trade carried by small sailing vessels, hugging the coastline, as their masters navigated by identifying landmarks.

In 1837 a Commission of Inquiry heard evidence that 'considerable plunder and disgraceful outrages take place frequently on the occurrence of wrecks along some parts of the coast' and ordered the Coastguard to furnish information on the subject. This was the first step to adding yet another duty – Receivership of Wrecks – to the Coastguard's other work.

When the Crimean War broke out in 1854, the country was, as usual, totally unprepared for a struggle with the colossal might of Imperial Russia, and the value of the Coastguard as a naval reserve was clearly shown. Every man who was available was drafted to the Fleet. It was no longer considered politically possible to continue the press-ganging of men, and men from the merchant fleet were invited to transfer to the fighting service but showed no enthusiasm.

They considered that they were already performing valuable service to the country by bringing in essential cargoes, and, in any case, they were better paid and had more comfortable quarters in the merchant ships.

Sir Charles Woods, in a Memorandum, described how in former times impressment forcibly diverted from the merchant service to that of the State the seamen who were required. 'The merchants had to provide for their wants by training other per-

A typical cliff rescue, Aberdeenshire (See chapter thirteen)

One of the most thrilling rescues of all time. French Trawler *Jeanne Gougy* wrecked off Land's End November 3rd 1962 (See chapter thirteen)

Saved from the French Trawler *Jeanne Gougy* wrecked off Land's End November 3rd 1962 (See chapter thirteen)

May 6, 1970. Trawler *Summerside* went ashore below cliffs near Aberdeen. Coastguard rescuers worked in waist-high icy surf to help crew over jagged rocks (See chapter thirteen)

sons or employing foreigners. It would be difficult except in the most pressing emergency, and certainly would be most undesirable to have recourse to impressment again. Since 1831 the men of the Coastguard have been seamen of good character discharged from ships and liable to serve in the Fleet when called upon. They have proved of the greatest use in forming the untrained crews of many of our ships'.

During the war, three thousand men of the Coastguard were drafted to the Fleet. The Revenue Cruisers were sent to intercept the enemy's shipping in the Channel and in this they were remarkably successful. Parliament was told in 1856 that the cruisers had captured eleven vessels and that eight had been condemned.

The vacant places in the coastguard were filled by pensioners and 'extra men'. These were civilians engaged for temporary service – a practice which had grown up over many years when men were absent from stations because of illness or other duties. It was often suspected that the extra men worked for smuggling gangs when they were not required to protect the revenue.

When the war was over and the Coastguard Act was being debated in Parliament, in 1856, it was stated that the Coastguard might have been more useful than they were if sufficient attention had been paid to rendering the service efficient in all its branches.

The Lieutenants appointed to the Coastguard had grown old in the service and many had become utterly incapable of performing any active duty. There had not been adequate inducement for young and active officers to enter the service, and as to one of the advantages which it was supposed might be derived from it by raising men for the navy it had failed altogether.

An Admiralty spokesman declared that the men had been good seamen but were too long in the coastguard service without naval refresher courses. They proposed to pension off the older men and replace them.

Admiral Sir Charles Napier said, in the debate, that the men of the Coastguard who served in his flagship were bald-headed and needed spectacles for reading but 'they were a fine example to the young men sent to sea without proper training, and were the steadiest men in the service'.

The Customs had serious objections about the Coastguard being drafted into the Navy, leaving them without a force for which they were required to foot the bill.

C

The successes of the revenue cruisers in intercepting Russian ships in the Channel was due to information supplied by British ambassadors and consular officials in neutral countries.

Lord Pakenham who was stationed in Lisbon reported, in a letter to the Earl of Clarendon, on 28th March 1854, that ten vessels under Russian colours had left the Tagus. He enclosed a letter from the British consul in Oporto which added the information that 'during the last six months four vessels arrived under the Russian flag and left under the Hanoverian flag without a change of master or crew'. The Ambassador's list of ships' names with others from intelligence officers were sent to the Comptroller-General who issued a memorandum listing fourteen Russian ships sailing under Hanoverian colours. Inspecting Commanders were instructed to order the commanders of the revenue cruisers to detain the vessels and take them into port.

Two weeks later Commander Grey Skipwith, Inspecting Commander of the Coastguard at Folkestone reported that one of his boats commanded by Lieutenant George Durbin had detained the Russian barque *Kamschatka* and sailed her to London docks. The ship, one of the ten reported from Lisbon, and its cargo was condemned and sold for £2,230 17s. 9d.

On 21st April 1854 a message was sent to Coastguard H.Q. from the Argus revenue cruiser, *Spithead*: Having during last night guarded the eastern entrance of the Wight with this steamer and a boat at a suspected spot inside; and nothing suspicious seen, I steamed out after daylight to the offing in search of smuggling craft, and to examine vessels likely to have on board contraband stores of war. At noon, after examining several vessels, I boarded the Russian barque *Froija* of Lisbon bound for the Baltic laden with salt; and I have detained her and towed her to this port. J. S. W. Grandy, Commander. The *Froija* was condemned and sold with her cargo for £3,144 15s. 0d.

Four days later H.M. Revenue Steamer *Argus* made another capture. Commander Grandy reported that while cruising between Beachy Head and the Owers he fell in with the Russian brig *Livonia* from Lisbon with salt, the property of the merchants of Riga. 'I detained her and towed her to Portsmouth'.

The *Livonia* was condemned and sold for £2,010.

Two days later on 27th April H.M. Revenue Cruiser *Petrel*

66

reported 'While cruising in the Channel in the cruiser under my command, yesterday at 11 a.m. St Catherine's Point, I boarded the Prussian barque *Fama* of Wasa from Sardinia, laden with salt, bound for some part of Russia as was first stated by the master John Ostman; afterwards the mate stated Elsinore, and after which they informed me they did not know where they were bound, being bound wherever they thought proper; I took charge of her and brought her to this port. John Hughes, Commander. Portsmouth.' The barque was sold for £2,418 8s. 9d.

The revenue cruiser *Lion* captured the Russian brigantine *Johannes,* from Cadiz bound for Elsinore with a cargo of salt, off Folkestone and towed it to Dover. The ship was sold for £854 6s. 0d.

This brought the total captures in one week to four and deprived the Russians if not of contraband stores of war, of a large quantity of salt. Before the war ended the enemy had lost another seven vessels to the revenue cruiser patrols, again mainly loaded with salt.

The end of the Crimean war brought criticism of the Navy's recruiting methods, and it was made clear in political circles that the people would no longer countenance such crude methods as the pressgang. In any case the ships had become too sophisticated in weaponry and manoeuvres to be efficiently manned by un-trained sailors.

The Coastguards, although trained seamen, were out of touch with the latest developments in the Fleet, but they were a ready reserve which had stood the country in good stead in an emergency.

The Admiralty was anxious to gain complete control of such a valuable source of manpower, and proposed that the service should be transferred to naval control and trained as a Fleet Reserve.

Rumours of the existence of this plan reached the Board of Customs in June 1856 and the reaction was immediate. In a letter to the Treasury, the Board declared 'We understand that a Bill is about to be introduced into Parliament having as its object the transfer of the Coastguard from this Department and to place the same entirely under the directions of the Lords Commissioners of the Admiralty, and, being of the opinion that the measure, if carried into effect, cannot fail to be productive of serious consequences to the Revenue . . .' But the Board was overruled.

The Coastguard Service Act – An Act to Provide for the Better Defence of the Coasts of the Realm, and the more ready Manning of the Navy, and to Transfer to the Admiralty the Government of the Coastguard – was passed through Parliament, and received the Royal Assent on 29th July 1856.

On 2nd August the Treasury replied to the Customs letter 'The responsibility of this change rests entirely with Her Majesty's Government, and, having fully stated your objections you will stand entirely exonerated if any of the inconveniences which you apprehense should arise to the detriment of the Public Service'.

The Coastguard was transferred to the Admiralty on 1st October 1856.

This was the act by which the old coastguard service with all its traditions and historical associations with smuggling finally officially disappeared.

On paper, however, the anti-smuggling tradition was recognized by instructions that the mounted guard at Coastguard stations was to be recruited from cavalry regiments to patrol the lanes at night and search out regular smugglers' landing places. Each station was allowed £7 per annum for candles and fuel oil for official purposes. A detached watch-house received 25/- per quarter in winter and £1 a quarter in summer for fuel.

Where a station was remote from a church the Chief Officer was required to hold services on Sundays at the station.

Any member of the service guilty of collusion with smugglers was to be dismissed; fined and prevented for ever from serving the Crown in any capacity.

Extra duties introduced included the requirement that all coastguards were to render all possible assistance to vessels in distress, and to wrecks. For salvage purposes the Chief Officers were to obtain a certificate from the master of a vessel, setting out the services rendered.

In 1862 Sir Thomas Fremantle, Chairman of the Board of Customs, told a Select Committee on the Inland Revenue and Customs Establishments that the Coastguard was looked upon strictly in the light of a Naval Reserve. He had no control over the service.

The coastguard employed its men for the prevention of smuggling and watching the coast generally, while the Customs officer was responsible for preventing smuggling by vessels entering the creek where he was located.

Mr M. Daly, a Customs examining officer from Liverpool giving evidence before the same committee thought it was difficult to form an opinion on the value of the Coastguard for the prevention of smuggling but he thought it hardly did to any great extent. 'There is only one efficient method of preventing smuggling and that is by a reduction of duty so that it will not be worth a man's while to smuggle. As long as you keep up a rate on tobacco which is equivalent to 600 or 700% it will be necessary to have a very numerous coastguard to prevent the article from being smuggled'.

The Coastguard had always performed some duties in connection with wreck, salvage and lifesaving apparatus, and, by an instruction of 1866 they were authorized to take an active part in the working of lifeboats. Another duty became the reporting on movements of buoys, beacons and light vessels. The list continued to grow as the years passed.

5
Gubby Ships and Hulks

The Coastguard Squadron which included some of the famous men-o'-war, pride of the Royal Navy in the days of sail, had the revenue cruisers attached as tenders. These fine old ships were posted to the main ports round the coast, where their names and exploits were proudly remembered.

They were obsolete when the first naval gun fired a shell, and it was quickly realized that such guns, and, engines not sail were essential to survival in battle. The wooden ships needed protection from high velocity shells and naval warfare was revolutionized. The day of the ironclad had dawned.

H.M.S. *Cornwallis*, 1,800 tons, launched at Bombay in 1813 became coastguard ship in the Humber. She had played an important part in the American war and served later on the China station. She carried 347 officers and men, and was converted to steam and reduced to sixty guns in 1855.

In 1857, after service in the Crimean war, she arrived in the Humber where she remained as coastguard ship for seven years. She was then condemned as unserviceable and fit only for firewood. However, she was saved from such an ignominious end when a jetty at Sheerness required enlarging. Her superstructure was cut down and she was beached. The deck was cemented over and she was soon known to the people of Sheerness as Cornwallis Jetty.

H.M.S. *Pembroke,* stationed at Harwich was another man-o'-war built in 1813 and reduced to sixty guns when she was fitted with engines. After service with the coastguard she sailed to Chatham where she was flagship, and the naval depot there later bore her name.

The *Blenheim,* another of the 1813 vessels, also converted to steam, took part in the Baltic expedition where she landed her guns for the battle of Bomarsund. She went to Weymouth as coastguard ship until scrapped in 1865.

The most famous of the coastguard ships was H.M.S. *Eagle,* of 2,340 tons, stationed at Milford Haven. Built at Northfleet in 1804 at the request of Admiral Lord Nelson, who demanded the construction of seventy-four-gun ships to strengthen his fleet. Immediately after being fitted out she sailed to the Mediterranean and went into action in 1806. She had an exceptionally high turn of speed and captured many enemy vessels, earning her crew large sums in prize money.

In 1831 she was cut down to fifty guns, and went to Milford Haven in 1858. A few years later she was posted to Southampton as a drill ship for the Naval Reserve. Later she moved to the Mersey where she was R.N.R. and R.N.V.R. drill ship until 1926, under the name of H.M.S. *Eaglet.*

Eagle's predecessor in the Mersey, in 1857 was H.M.S. *Hastings,* another seventy-four, built in India in 1818 for the East India Company and bought from the company by the Royal Navy the following year. She was converted to steam in 1854 and saw service in the second Baltic expedition of the Crimean war in 1855. Her engines were removed in 1868 when she was converted into a coastguard hulk, and she ended her days, as firewood, in 1886.

The coastguard ship at Queensferry was H.M.S. *Lord Warden,* and Admiral the Hon. Sir Edmund R. Fremantle, G.C.B., described life on the ship when he was her commander for over two years.

He was appointed in May 1877 while he was attending a torpedo course at Portsmouth.

'I had a sudden order to join the *Lord Warden* immediately and take her to sea, in consequence of the ill-health of her captain. She had only recently been commissioned and winter time and a reduced complement of officers and men were not factors tending to good man-o'-warlike appearance or discipline.

'Captain Bedingfeld who had commissioned her had retired, being succeeded by Captain C. Buckle who had known the *Lord Warden* in tip-top order as flagship in the Mediterranean. He was in bad health and unable to put matters to rights, while he deeply felt the contrast between the ship as he had known her previously and her state when he joined. Accordingly when he knew that she must go to sea, he applied to remain ashore on leave.

'The *Lord Warden* was a fine old ironclad of 7,800 tons and

71

a fair steamer. She and her sister the *Lord Clyde* were the only wooden ironclad battle ships built in England.

'Two days after I joined, we sailed to join the Channel Squadron at Plymouth, calling at Humber, Yarmouth and Sheerness to pick up coastguardsmen to fill up our complement.

'At the end of this cruise we were detained south, first as guardship at Cowes and then for docking and overhaul at Portsmouth. We did not leave Portsmouth for our station till October 1877, after five month's absence from the Coastguard District under my orders.

'The command of a coastguard ship meant that the Captain was in charge of a "district" of Coastguard. In my case this meant all the stations on the east coast of Scotland, and even Loch Inver on the west coast, besides the Orkneys and Shetlands. All these stations had to be inspected once a year, besides the Royal Naval Reserve drill ships at Dundee, Aberdeen and Inverness, and drill batteries at other stations.

'My beat was extensive, but the men were few, only 175 or 185 altogether, so that a big ship like the *Lord Warden* had to fill up from other coastguard districts. The ships had only half complements when at their stations, but as they only went to sea to fire once a quarter, it was supposed that this did not matter, and when the summer cruise of four to six weeks took place, extra officers were appointed and the crew completed.

'It certainly was simple to exist in a slovenly condition but far from an easy task to keep up man-o'-war discipline and order. Hence the opprobrious name of "Gobby Ships" or "Gobbies" as they were commonly called. Naturally they were not popular with the best officers and men, and the officers only counted "harbour time" that is three years for two years "sea service" towards promotion or retirement, which was a real grievance.

'Under these circumstances much depended on the captain, and he had a choice of evils as regards executive officers; indifferent ones he might keep, but good ones only came for a time until something better turned up. As I preferred the latter I had in my two and a half years in command of the *Lord Warden*, three commanders, three first lieutenants and three chief engineers. So what with absence inspecting, short complements, and officers constantly changing, it was hard indeed to prevent a coastguard ship from earning the right to the slang name "gobby".

'However there were compensations. I lived on shore in a house close to the ship, and the heads of departments were generally efficient men, but I think most of them considered the *Lord Warden* as a harbour appointment in the light of a swindle, their families being at Portsmouth or Devonport, and even the six weeks leave a year to which they were entitled meant a good hole in their pockets for travelling expenses, which they could ill afford.

'In 1877, after our cruise with the Channel Squadron, the *Lord Warden* was ordered to be guardship at Cowes during the Cowes week, which I need scarcely say was generally appreciated, but "some were sad and felt no mirth" at being kept away from their port where they had established their families, and I remember the old staff commander John "Dan" O'Connell saying to me quite seriously, in the middle of all the gaiety and nautical excitement of the Cowes week that "this was worse than the coast of Africa."

'We had two trips each way, every year. First to Portsmouth to refit and dock then north again to fill up our crews, then south again for our yearly cruise and back to our station in August. At this time 1877-79 the sailing traditions still held good, and the *Lord Warden*, like the other ironclads of that date was a masted ship was a fair spread of canvas, but she was scarcely manageable under sail alone and it was a great feat to her to "wear" at all. Though a single screw ship she was very handy under steam, steering like a "jolly boat" in naval parlance. All men-o'-war at that time were supposed to have a "most economical rate of steaming" which had been carefully ascertained by numerous trials.

'The *Lord Warden* was a great coal eater and I always used sail as much as possible.

'In 1878 we formed a reserve squadron under Sir Cooper Key for four months, and it was a nice change having a full complement on board. Our cruises were generally off the coast of Ireland and in the Atlantic, but in 1879 we went to Gibraltar and cruised, under the orders of Lord John Hay, with the Channel Squadron. Altogether I found that I was rather over a year away from my station out of my two and a half years of command.

'The inspection of Coastguard Stations was one of my principal duties. We were away on the cruise in the summer, and both in

C*

'77 and '78 I did not return north till late in the year, so that most of my inspections were done in wintertime.

It was also the right time for the R.N.R. men many of whom were whalers and sealers who were at sea all the summer and did their drill in the winter. Thus at the Shetlands for instance there were 250-300 fine seamen on drill in midwinter and the battery was closed in summer.

'I had a splendid Chief Officer of Coastguard in charge of the drill battery at Lerwick, a Mr Johnson who drilled capitally and it was a pleasure to make a trip to the Ultima Thule to support him. These men were of good Norse breed, though they spoke little English and were supposed to think more of their retainer drill pay, which was a boon to them during the winter months, than the possibilities of war service. One difficulty was that in December and January there were only two or three hours of daylight so that an inspection began and ended in the dark.

'I used to go to the Shetlands either in a gunboat or by mail steamer from Granton. I rather enjoyed my inspections of the coastguard and I think I visited every station each year, chiefly by rail and driving, as landing from a gunboat could not be depended on. It was often very cold work and I have frequently inspected stations such as Peterhead and Wick in a snowstorm, wearing a frock coat as no greatcoats were uniform at that period, and it was important to insist on strict uniform, the tendency being to be decidedly slack in such matters.

'At that period a good many Chief Officers in charge of coastguard stations were old Customs men who knew more of the preventive service than of drill, and the naval authorities were anxious for them to retire, so that I am afraid I took rather a malicious pleasure in running them up and down the braes and generally making them feel their inefficiency, which was specially marked when they had to wear a frockcoat with the unusual encumbrance of a sword.

'My time was generally limited, and the boathouse was often some distance from the station and had to be kept locked. At one station, Rattrey Head, it was quite a mile away and I used to race there after inspecting all the men at the station, leaving the Chief Officer to follow as best he could.

'I remember my last visit, in November 1879, the Chief Officer, an old fellow called Mackinnon saying "Captain, I've got the

74

fastest runner in the detachment with the keys, and he'll run down as soon as you've inspected the station, and I don't think he'll be long after you and I'll follow".

'It was always important to see the boat and the boathouse, but in this instance I had built the boathouse on my own responsibility as it was much needed, "in anticipation of their Lordships' approval," which formed the subject of a long correspondence.

'On another occasion after I had made an old Chief Officer run about the station with me he naïvely told me a story how when in Ireland the Chief Officer at his station, after an active District Captain had been round, had said to him "Really Mr B. I think I must send in my papers, as I cannot stand this." But I says to him, "He only comes once a year and next year there will be another Captain who perhaps won't run you about so much, and so it turned out, for the next man never got out of his carriage."

'As this was most likely my last visit the story was decidedly applicable, and Mr B. did not offer to retire.

'One great question always was that of promotion and appointments and on this hinged the comfort of the men and their families, so that it was well to be acquainted with the wives and families of coastguardsmen, as promotion to a man with a family to a place where no schooling was to be had would be ruinous.

'I endeavoured as far as I could to make my promotions with due consideration for the men.

'When I first went to Queensferry, as the former guardship had been unfit to cruise, the coastguardsmen had not been to sea for some years and going afloat was unpopular, as the men's subsistence money which helped the family was stopped. Though this was rather a grievance, after the first year our men rather liked the change. They were fine men and good sailors though some had got rather stout for going aloft.

'Most of the coastguard had been petty officers but as "boatmen" they were only equivalent to ABs in the Navy, so that it was reasonable to humour them as much as possible. Certainly I never had any trouble with them, and with our coastguard men on board, the *Lord Warden* was in very good order and even smart aloft. Indeed I remember being very proud of the way we laid a sheet anchor out at Portland with four shackles of chain, when with the Reserve Fleet in 1878, on which we were complimented by our two Admirals Sir Cooper Key and Admiral Boys.

'The removal of coastguardsmen was effected rather cruelly. I had two gunboats *Tyrian* and *Netley* and two coastguard sailing cutters *Eagle* and *Squirrel,* all tenders to the *Lord Warden,* and, to save railway fares the changes of stations were generally effected through these craft, but in bad weather and wintertime a family might be on board a sailing cutter for several days. The officers made the women and children as comfortable as they could, but I confess to have seen a sailing cutter which had a family on board, beating up to the north near Montrose, in a snowstorm, which I think should be described as a method of barbarism.

'As District Captain my great object was to see that each Coastguard Station had its boat, boathouse and flagstaff, and I had much correspondence before I could get these necessaries provided.

'In Scotland where there were few regular coastguard stations, in many cases houses had to be hired so that I was in constant correspondence on the subject of houses for coastguardsmen.

'This was true in any question connected with money. The Admiralty executive, imbued with naval ideas, was little troubled with red tape, but the civilian branches of the Admiralty belong to the great circumlocution office, full of precedents and good reasons for asking for further information, but reluctant to come to a decision.

'I considered that a small cruiser would be useful in the Firth of Forth when the guardship was away, and the tenders were protecting the fisheries in the summer.

'I looked round and came across a suitable little cutter-yacht, of seventeen tons, at Dundee, which was offered to me for £120 fully equipped. Accordingly I applied for leave to buy her for the Coastguard Service. Several letters having received no answer, I at last telegraphed asking for a reply to my letters. To this wire I got a prompt answer informing me that the telegraph should only be used in urgent and important cases, and that this did not come under such a category.

'As I was determined not to lose the boat, I at once accepted her and, pending a further decision, I was allowed man her with three men. The correspondence was almost interminable and I quite expected to have to pay for her myself, at one time, but eventually the purchase was approved. I named her the *Psyche,* and I was rather amused to see her mentioned in the First Lord's speech in moving the Navy Estimates, with two or three other small craft, as an item in a sum of £150,000.

'Many of our stations were much scattered, with detachments from the parent station miles away, but I think Wick took the cake in this respect. We had two detachments at Loch Inver and Tongue, of two men each, some seventy to eighty miles from the parent station and nearly fifty miles from any railway. It is of Tongue on the northern coast I would speak.

'I used to visit it either from Lairg or Thurso where the railway ended, the distance being fifty miles from Lairg and rather less from Thurso. There were two men on detachment at Tongue, the senior of whom, a man named Condon, a commissioned boatman-in-charge. Condon was a reliable man who had been a gunner's mate in the service, but he was a Roman Catholic, which did not add to his popularity, and he took rather a sombre view of life.

'It was in the spring of 1879, I saw Condon at Waverley Station, Edinburgh, on his return home after doing his drill in the *Lord Warden.* He was not coming for the cruise that year but his colleague was, and he seemed rather unhappy at the prospect of being alone while we were away. So, partly to cheer him up, I called him and told him that he would have a fine chance of distinction this year, of which I was sure he would avail himself, that a French lugger the *Amelie,* which had been about Loch Errriboll last year, was sure to come again to sell brandy, and that I relied on him to capture her if he could.

'I did not really think he could do this singlehanded, but that he might do so with assistance from Wick. He promised to keep a good lookout for the smuggler, and seemed much pleased.

'He kept his word, for with the assistance of some half-hearted Reserve men, he seized the *Amelie,* and almost alone, kept possession of her for thirty-six hours, till he could get assistance.

'The Frenchman had heard of the coastguard and had a loaded blunderbuss on deck which he boasted he would use against him, if any attempt was made to interfere with his business. He afterwards complained that Condon, who had been lying down in a boat owned by a fisherman, had jumped on board and seized him by the throat, putting his sword to his stomach. "Which he did not consider English fash".'

The smuggler was condemned and of course, Condon got promotion and a share in the seizure. It was really a very plucky act, isolated as he was, with the sympathies of the population entirely with the smuggler who had given them cheap brandy without Customs dues.

Admiral Fremantle was himself a brave man, and he received the Copper Medal of the Royal Humane Society for rescuing a boy who fell from the rigging, broke his arm, and was in danger of drowning.

'I feared he would be drowned before a boat could reach him, as he was drifting astern, so I jumped from the poop with all my clothes on, and had little difficulty in saving him' he wrote later. 'It was an easy thing to do, though I spoilt a valuable gold watch, but it got into the papers and the Admiral, Sir Beauchamp Seymour called on me to report it, and I was awarded the medal'.

Although the Coastguard Service was land-based, if there were no suitable quarters on shore, and in some cases for reasons of economy, the men were housed in Watch-vessels, or hulks, which ranged from a small sloop at Harwick to old men-o'-war on the Kent and Sussex coasts, and in the Thames estuary. This was a most unpopular posting and, after two years' service in a hulk, the men were moved to a good station as compensation. Some of the old hulks were still in use at the beginning of the present century.

One of these was the frigate H.M.S. *Cadmus,* one of the biggest ships in the service. She was moored in the River Swale, twenty yards from the shore and accommodated seven men with their families – six wives and eleven children, and the Commanding Officer. She was replaced by a shore station in 1903.

A Contemporary account of life on the ship gives some idea of the hardship involved.

The upper deck was tarred over to keep out the weather, and the mess deck was fitted out with cabins. These had flimsy partitions which meant that all matrimonial discussions had to be in whispers if the entire crew were not to be the recipients of family confidences.

Each family was allocated two or three cabins, according to

its size. One was used as a living-room and the others as sleeping quarters. These had one large bunk in each with a cupboard under it. The living-room had a hinged table attached to the bulkhead and a small stove for warmth.

The wives cooked for their families on a communal stove, which was cleaned each day and relit by the morning duty watch. He set all the family kettles to boil before waking the wives to cook breakfast. The single men had to rely on the married women to cook for them.

The commanding officer had his own galley, but it was the custom to boil his morning kettle with the others, a privilege for which he paid five shillings a month for the coal.

Every man was allowed fourpence a day for coal and lighting. The washing was done on a rota system, governed by seniority which had to be approved by the Commanding Officer. As each wife had a day allotted and the portable boiler was on the top deck, the ship had a permanent unnaval appearance as there was always a line of 'smalls' flapping in the breeze.

Faversham was at that time a busy port into which sailed large numbers of Norwegian timber-carrying ships. It was also a haven for the local fishing fleet.

All these ships had to be carefully watched, and the men of the *Cadmus* were mainly engaged in boarding and searching vessels. The Coastguards had to remain on board until Customs officers took over at the dock, and this could be a long and uncomfortable duty.

Known as 'tide-waiting', the ships lay at anchor for up to a week waiting for the spring tides to give them sufficient water to get up the Swale to Faversham. The ships' captains were usually kindly men but they had no accommodation for passengers, and the poor coastguards could at best expect the loan of a blanket, and a diet of salt fish and hardtack.

All the ship's boats had to be kept ready for launching at a moment's notice to give chase and board any vessels that failed to acknowledge signals from the *Cadmus,* or if they appeared to be smugglers. One man was on watch at all times on the forecastle ready to call out the crew when necessary.

For most duties the crew used a fourteen feet long punt unless the water was too rough, when they launched one of the bigger whalers.

The wives were allowed to land on Fridays and Saturdays, to do the weekly shopping for their families, but there was no shore leave for recreation. One man acted as ship's postman and was rowed ashore each day to take letters to Faversham and collect the mail.

While he was away two of his colleagues rowed the 'waterboat' loaded with empty casks to the river bank where there was a pump. They filled up with fresh water and ferried the casks to the hulk before returning to collect the postman.

All hands were allowed to go to the galley for one hour each night, for a singsong, but from 8 p.m. there had to be complete silence throughout the ship.

As the *Cadmus* was moored three miles from Faversham even by the shortest route across the marshes, and in any case no boat was available to take them ashore, the children had no formal education. The wives organized their own 'school' but as none were teachers the children learned little theory but gained plenty of practical knowledge of ships, sailors and the sea.

The monotony of life in these small isolated communities was broken occasionally by visits from friends made by the wives during their shopping expeditions, or when relatives could be persuaded to stay. One of the few privileges allowed the men of the hulks. It required extraordinary knowledge of human nature on the part of the commanding officer to prevent the friction between the families from disrupting the community. The crews were made up, in the main, by men undergoing punishment or by recruits under training, and, understandably there was a saying in the service that any coastguard station was better than a watch-vessel.

6
Signallers and Life-savers

From its earliest days signalling was the forte of the Coastguard Service, and it was this skill that was of greatest value to the Naval Reserve.

Signal exercises were constantly carried out and, at the War Signal Stations there were two drills daily. In the morning the men were exercised using semaphore flags and telegraphy, and, at night with flashing lamps.

The day before the naval manoeuvres began in August, 1890 the Coastguard Signal Stations were mobilized and thoroughly tested a new method of passing intelligence reports. The tests were completely successful, due entirely to the efficiency of the men – as it was later proved that their equipment was obsolete.

It was therefore decided that the stations should be linked by the Post Office telegraphic system, and that signal stations should be established on the west coast, in Ireland, and Scotland, equipped with semaphore equipment similar to that provided on the south and east coasts of England.

This took time and for some years the only line of communication between stations was by passing letters from hand to hand when patrols met.

The Coastguard was one of the first official services to be equipped with the telephone, and, in 1892 a System of Coast Communications was built up under the G.P.O., with nearly all Coastguard Stations to which Life-saving Apparatus was supplied, or which were situated at places where lifeboats were stationed, connected by telephone to the Coastguard Stations on either side. Soon a line was installed right round the coast.

The scheme started after the Royal National Lifeboat Association drew attention, in 1891, to the 'want of means of conveying information of the need for lifeboats between signal stations and lifeboat stations'. On 26th April 1892 the House of Commons passed a resolution, on the motion by Sir Edward Birkbeck 'That with a view to the better prevention of loss of life and property in cases of vessels in distress or shipwrecked on the coast of the United Kingdom, and to give the earliest possible information to Lifeboat authorities and Rocket Apparatus Stations, in the opinion of this House it is desirable that all Coastguard Stations on the sea coast, and Signal Stations, should be telephonically or telegraphically connected by the Government, and that on those parts of the coast when such stations do not exist, the Post Offices nearest to the Lifeboat Stations be so connected'.

All coastguard stations in a district were connected on the same line, and each had a code of rings. There were strict orders that no one was to listen in on conversations.

In isolated areas the coastguard was allowed to receive telegrams for the local villagers, and to pass them on to the Post Office for delivery.

Post Offices were closed from 8 p.m. to 8 a.m. and, on Sundays all day, except between 8–10 a.m., and some difficulty was encountered in securing attention to calls on the lifesaving service. To deal with this a call-bell system was introduced whereby bells were installed in the bedroom of the local Postmaster or other officer of the post office. These officials were paid 30/- a year for having the bell in their bedroom and 5/- to 7/6d. for answering each call, depending on whether they had to leave the house to attend to the call.

Where possible the coastguard stations were switched through to the nearest larger post office which was manned during the night. Call-bells were placed in some police stations, and the policeman on duty went round and roused the telegraphist who hurried to the post office to receive or transmit the message.

A new instruction was added to the Coastguard Orders pointing out that it 'is the duty of the Coastguard to give constant attendance at the coast communications telephones, and they are on no account to be left unattended by them on the lifesaving apparatus being called out, unless it is impossible to complete the Lifesaving Apparatus crew from other sources, when a competent person (preferably the wife of one of the Coastguardsmen) may be engaged for the duty and paid'.

This instruction remained in force into the late 1960s.

The signal stations were located on headlands and at river estuaries overlooking busy shipping routes, and Coastguards undertook signalling on behalf of Lloyds of London, for which payment was made at rates from 5/- to 34/- a week. At Sandgate they received 3d a message for reporting ocean-going steamers, and 5/- a week for reporting all vessels passing the Smalls lighthouse.

With the advent of wireless telegraphy, the Coastguard was quickly in the field, and in 1902 six stations were equipped and had trained operators. These were at Dover, Culver, Portland, Rame Head, Scilly and Roche Point. These stations were so successful that eight more were equipped in the following year.

In his report on giving up command of the Coastguard in 1905, Admiral Ernest Rice stated that the strength was 4,091 officers and men, and that the force was being increased to the approved total of 4,500 to meet the requirements of new Signal Stations and Wireless Telegraph Stations.

There was no lack of candidates for the service, and on 26th January 1905 there were 559 applicants and only 130 vacancies.

Admiral Rice observed that all men entering the coastguard were required to undergo a preliminary course of signalling, and that proposals were under consideration to further increase the efficiency of the signal stations by keeping more of them manned in peacetime. All the signal and wireless telegraph stations were placed in charge of a Lieutenant (T) belonging to the Admiral's staff, with a Signal Boatswain as his assistant.

A new substantive rank of Station Signalman was established for Boatmen and Commissioned Boatmen, with a special allowance of 2d per day. A special allowance of 1/6d a day was paid to the Torpedo Instructor allotted to each station for taking charge of the W/T equipment.

The number of coastguardsmen employed full time at the War Signal Stations in peacetime was increased to 133, and they were known as Assistant Station Signalmen.

The Admiral, ever conscious of the navy reserve role of the coastguard, pointed out that these additional men were, when relieved by pensioners, available on mobilization to be sent to the general naval depots where they would form a valuable addition to the number of men afloat with a knowledge of signals.

In 1905, in addition to the W/T Stations already established, ten others were building at Ducansby Head, Fraserburgh, Tynemouth, Cleethorpes, Winterton (Yarmouth), Tiree, Slyne Head, Dunmore Head, St Ann's and Port Patrick. Lloyds had established five W/T Stations, worked by coastguards, at Brow Head, Malin Head, Butt of Lewis, St Abb's Head and St Catherine's Point. These stations were included in the Admiralty's 'Scheme of Defence'.

Wireless stations were also established at Alderney, Guernsey and Jersey. The Jersey and Guernsey stations had equipment supplied by the War Office and were worked for the War Office by the coastguard. This made a total of twenty-five stations in the United Kingdom worked by coastguards.

The men at the Admiralty W/T Stations at Dover, Scilly, Roche Point and St Ann's received commercial reports for Lloyds.

Admiral Rice was concerned at the difficulty in training and practice at the stations and he pointed out that in 1903 the average work done with H.M. Ships was one word a day. This had risen to one message a day by 1905. As regular daily exercises in exchanging messages with passing ships was essential to efficiency, he considered that the best way to obtain this was to encourage commercial work by the coastguardsmen who would be operators at the stations in wartime.

The admiral was a shrewd man and anticipating that such a suggestion would be vetoed by the Admiralty, he proposed that it should be accepted in principle that any commercial company for whom the work was done by the coastguard at Admiralty and other stations should pay 'a reasonable sum yearly towards the working expense of the station'.

The reasonable sum was negotiated and later written into the Coastguard Regulations in 1913.

War Signal Stations performing Lloyds work with a view to keeping the stations fully exercised received the following payments, which were shared amongst the men doing the work.

    Signalling:
        Day-work 10/- per week.
        Day and night work £1 per week.
    Telegraphy:
        Day-work 7/- per week.
        Day and night work 14/- per week.

The cash was divided two shares to the officer or petty officer in charge and one share to each member of the crew for signalling work, and one share to each operator for telegraphic work.

Special arrangements were made for a night watch to be kept for reporting special vessels, whenever Lloyds telegraphed to a station. Lloyds paid 2/6d to the crew for each night that such a watch was kept.

The first official reference connecting the coastguard with life-saving duties is contained in a single article of the Coastguard Instructions of 1841 which stated: 'It is the duty of the officers and crews of the cruisers and coastguard stations to render all possible assistance to vessels in distress; and in cases of ship-wrecks to use their utmost endeavours to save the lives of the persons on board, and to save and protect from plunder and em-bezzlement the rigging, sails, stores and cargo'.

Following the transfer of the coastguard to the Admiralty in 1856 there were no further references to life-saving duties and it was clear that the Admiralty did not accept direct responsi-bility for such duties. This is shown in Article 654 of the Admiralty Coastguard Instructions of 1911, which states: 'It is to be noted that the Admiralty does not accept responsibility for any inadequacy of the system of life-saving arrangements that may exist in any portion of the coasts of the United Kingdom, but, at places where Coastguardsmen are stationed, such Coast-guardsmen are to render every possible assistance to the local life-saving services as far as is compatible with their proper duties'.

In an attempt to fill the gap in these life-saving services a number of private life-saving corps were formed in the first half of the nineteenth century, and, under the provisions of the Mer-chant Shipping Act 1854, the Board of Trade took over the supervision and management of these companies, and, gradually provided further Life-saving Apparatus Companies all round the coast.

The position was anomalous: the Admiralty was responsible for the Coastguard Service, and the Board of Trade for the pro-vision of a life-saving service, but, although the Board of Trade was responsible for the supervision and direction of the work of the Rocket Life-saving Apparatus Companies and Brigades, they were dependent in the main for the effectiveness of this work on assistance given by the Coastguard.

The early history of the Volunteer Life-saving Brigades on the north-east coast is of interest as they were the forerunners of the modern Auxiliary Coastguard Service.

The Tynemouth Volunteer Life Brigade was formed in 1865, and, on 31st January 1866 a second Brigade was formed at South Shields which was accepted by the Board of Trade under the same terms as the Tynemouth Brigade.

The first drill was held on 17th February 1866 under the supervision of Mr Byrne, Chief Officer of Coastguard at Tynemouth, with the assistance of the Tynemouth Brigade.

The brigade consisted of four divisions, split into seven sections, and a drill card of the period details the allocation of men and jobs.

Division one:
> Section one: six men: provide rocket frame, tube box and rockets and attend to signal.
> Section two: eight men: provide two rocket lines; four men to a box.

Division two:
> Section three: 6-26 men: provide whip line (in coils) tail block and metal tallies, and tend whip.

Division three:
> Section four: 2-4 men: provide breeches buoy and chair; reeve the hawser through the buoy or chair block and bend whip to block.
> Section five: 16-44 men: provide hawser; pass end under whip. Use anchor and tackles as directed.

Division four:
> Section six: 2-12 men: provide cork jackets and lifelines and look out for people arriving from wreck.
> Section seven: Remainder: Keep the ground clear for proper working of gear.

It was this Brigade that, after only three practice drills, was the first of these officially recognized organizations to save life.

On 2nd April 1866 the schooner *Tenterden* of Sunderland went ashore behind the South Pier. Three guns were fired from the Spanish Battery as a signal to call out the Brigade, and forty-five members hurried to the scene where, under the supervision of the Coastguard, they rescued the seven man crew, and the captain's wife and baby. Mother and child were first to be brought ashore and this inspired an artist to paint a picture, entitled 'Saved', showing the fainting woman with the child tied in a blanket in her arms being held in the breeches buoy by a gallant lifesaver.

When mustering in bad weather the Brigade members had to find what shelter they could in the lee of buildings at the foot of the pier, and it was soon realized that a cabin was urgently needed to provide a lookout and also some degree of comfort. Plans were prepared but the work had not started when the brigade was severely tested by a gale which blew up on 5th January 1867.

In the evening a vessel went ashore close to the harbour. The alarm was given, but the guns could scarcely be heard above the fury of the gale, and at first only the members living close at hand turned out. They had barely completed the rescue of the crew when another craft was wrecked a mile to the south, followed by a third and then a fourth.

By morning the volunteers, soaked to the skin, were cold, hungry and exhausted, but they could look back with pride on a magnificent night's work. From the four ships they had saved nineteen lives and only two were lost.

This night's work brought swift action to provide a watch-house.

An appeal was launched, land was granted by the Tyne Improvement Commission and, by October 1867 the first Brigade House was opened.

A contemporary report described the interior thus: 'It is elaborately fitted up; scarcely a comfort is wanting. The first impression that strikes you on entering is the completeness and compactness of the place. Every corner is ornamented with some useful article; here a cupboard containing restoratives, there a barometer, overhead is suspended a row of warm flannel drawers and stockings. Hanging on the walls are a number of oilskins and sou'westers. Down the entire centre of the room are neatly grained wood tables.

'In the middle stands a first-rate metal stove which throws a

87

comfortable heat through the whole building. In one corner a crimson curtain is suspended, behind which every now and then members look with their spy-glasses. Adjoining the lookout house is an excellently fitted up bathroom about eighteen feet long.

'At each end there are cosy bunks fitted with mattresses, blankets and rugs. In one corner there is a neatly fitted-up surgery'.

In the first ten years of its existence the Brigade saved eighty-eight lives. One of the more amusing incidents occurred when the schooner *Impulse* was driven ashore on the South Pier on 27th September 1868. The Brigade turned out but the crew showed no intention of coming ashore. Seven hours later when the wind and sea increased, and at the request of the crew, the apparatus was rigged and the crew of seven were brought ashore. The last man to leave the ship was the cook who came ashore carrying a steaming hot plum duff which he had been making.

On 9th December 1864, four days after the founding of the Tynemouth Brigade a letter was received from the Vicar of Whitley Bay saying that the men of Cullercoats (a small fishing village a mile north of the Tyne) would be most glad to co-operate in the movement. 'We propose to form a Cullercoats' Brigade of some of the best and steadiest men in the place who will be ready at any time to go out with the rocket apparatus which is left there'.

This brigade was in being early in 1865 and was the second enrolled in the United Kingdom. It mustered sixty to seventy members, the majority of them fishermen.

Their first rescue was on 9th December 1870. Shortly after 6 p.m. a barque was reported ashore on the Long Sands. The Brigade cart was manned and went to the scene. The Cullercoats' brigade fired a rocket over the vessel without effect, and the Tynemouth brigade which had arrived also fired a rocket but missed the target. The Cullercoats men fired the third rocket and took off nine members of the crew. The barque was the *City of Bristol* of South Shields.

The Tynemouth brigade gained international fame in 1901 when they saved a shipwrecked Russian sailor, with help from the Coastguard. Three members of the brigade, three coastguardsmen and a civilian nearly lost their lives in the operation, and, were later presented with silver medals by the Russian Government, and with diplomas signed by the Empress.

Reference has been made to the Rocket Life-saving Apparatus supplied by the Board of Trade. The history of the development of the rockets goes back even before the days of the Coast Blockade.

Sergeant John Bell, who was born on 1st March 1747 in Carlisle, joined the Royal Artillery in 1765. He was a keen inventor of a variety of objects including a crane; a harpoon; a petard and, a mortar to fire a lifeline ashore.

He was awarded £50 for his lifesaving device by the Society for the Encouragement of Arts, Manufactures and Commerce, in 1792, and published the result of a demonstration he gave before the Society at Woolwich on 29th August 1791.

Bell's mortar was designed to fire an eight-inch shell to which a line was attached. For the demonstration the mortar, weighing about six hundred-weights, was mounted on a boat moored 250 yards from the shore. The mortar was loaded and a fifteen-ounce powder charge fired the shell and line to a point 150 feet above the high water mark. The weight of the shell – seventy-five pounds – was sufficient to allow two men on an improvised raft to pull themselves ashore by the attached line without dragging the shell.

Although the experiment was a success, the idea was not exploited, and it is George William Manby who is credited with the invention of the first life-saving apparatus. His mortar which was similar in design to Bell's was intended to be fired from shore to ship.

A Committee of Parliament which examined Manby's petition for the adoption of his mortar reported, in 1810, that 'The invention of Mr Sergeant Bell in 1791, though ingenious, had in no instance produced any beneficial advantage, and it appears to this Committee that it is totally inapplicable in the case of vessels being stranded, the sea in such cases breaking over them in such a way as would prevent a shell firing to shore'. However, in 1815, Bell's daughter was voted £500 by Parliament in recognition of her father's invention.

Captain George Manby who was born in 1765 at Denver Hall, near Downham Market, Norfolk, went to school at Downham

Market where his school-fellow was Horatio Nelson, with whom he maintained a lifelong friendship. He completed his education at the Royal Military Academy, Woolwich, and intended joining the Artillery but the delay in obtaining a commission sent him to the Cambridgeshire Militia in which he reached the rank of Captain.

When he was eighteen years old he borrowed a mortar and smuggled it into Downham churchyard. There he attached a rope to the shot and fired it over the church, much to the indignation of the parson. After this escapade no further tests were attempted and the idea was shelved for twenty-four years.

Years later Manby bought a house overlooking the sea at Great Yarmouth, and it was on 18th February 1807 when the brig *Snipe* ran aground sixty yards off the Yarmouth beach that he remembered his early experiment. With a group of spectators he stood helpless while sixty-seven men perished a stone's throw from the beach, and he then determined that some method must be devised to effect rescues in similar circumstances in the future.

Manby wrote to the Board of Ordnance asking for the loan of a $5\frac{1}{2}$-in. mortar for experimental purposes.

After several failures, he found a method of attaching a line to the shot with platted rawhide strips, and, in August 1807 he demonstrated his invention to the Suffolk Humane Society.

On 12th February 1808, a year after the *Snipe* disaster, the brig *Elizabeth* went ashore on the same part of the beach and the crew were seen lashing themselves to the rigging, with the waves breaking over them. Manby took his mortar to the beach and with his first shot threw a line across the brig. The crew hauled on the line which took out a heavier rope, and seven members of the crew were saved.

In the same year that Manby conceived the idea of a life-saving mortar (1807), a rocket was proposed by Henry Trengrouse of Helston, Cornwall.

Trengrouse's rocket which was intended to be fired from ship or shore, was more accurate than Manby's mortar, but it was a remarkable coincidence that, unknown to one another, the two men were at the same time, designing methods of rescuing the shipwrecked by using a line and hawser to bring them ashore in a chair or cradle.

The rocket was fired from an ordinary musket by clipping on a pipe to house the charge, which had a line attached to the rocket-stick. It was fitted so that when the musket was fired the flash ignited the rocket primer.

This method had several advantages over the cumbersome mortar. There was less danger of the line snapping as the rocket took off slowly and accelerated away, but with the mortar there was an immediate shock of discharge. Size, too, was an advantage, the rocket could be packed in a box measuring four-feet-three-inches by one-foot-six.

The frigate *Anson* was wrecked in Mounts Bay, Cornwall in 1807 with the loss of the captain and one hundred members of his crew, and seventeen years later a print was published showing how the Trengrouse apparatus would have been used. It bore the comment 'the experiments made with this apparatus before official committees clearly exhibited its efficiency, as well as superiority both of which were officially reported. But the great superiority of Mr Trengrouse's method of forming a rope communication by means of a rocket was most eminently demonstrated recently at the Isle of Wight, when a line was carried over a wreck by the first essay of a rocket, in a most admirable manner, after the Manby mortar had failed in repeated efforts'.

Eleven years after the *Anson* disaster, Trengrouse demonstrated his rocket before Admiral Sir Charles Rowley and a Government Committee which reported 'Mr Trengrouse's model appears to be the best that has yet been suggested for the purpose of saving lives from shipwreck'.

It soon proved necessary to improve the power and range of the rockets and this problem was solved by Captain Edward Mourrier Boxer, who was Superintendent of the Royal Laboratory at Woolwich Arsenal, where he invented the Boxer Shrapnel Shell, the Boxer Portfire for use with life-saving apparatus, and, the Boxer Rocket which continued to be used as the main armament of the Life-saving Apparatus for over eighty years.

The principle of the rocket was a double charge. The first carried the projectile to its full elevation, and the second igniting during flight gave added impetus. The body of the rocket consisted of two cylinders of Bessemer sheet steel fixed end to end. Each was filled with a slow-burning composition, but a conical central cavity was left for quick and even burning. When prepared for firing a nine-feet six-inch stick was inserted through two square lugs on the head and base of the rocket.

The Boxer rocket was superseded by the Rescue Rocket in 1948.

The Rescue Rocket, fired by cordite, was developed for line-carrying and other service requirements during World War II, and these developments led to the decision to replace the Boxer for Coastguard work.

The end of the Boxer rockets and the introduction of the modern rescue rocket has been described by Commander J. J. Lewty, O.B.E., R.N.(Retd), Chief Inspector of Coastguard until his retirement in 1962. He recalled that soon after the end of World War II the Coastguard Headquarters received an ever increasing number of reports of erratic behaviour of Boxer rockets. Some apparently went in every direction except the desired one. There was even one report of an old gentlemen in a wheel-chair who had been watching a drill and was chased up the road by the rocket.

On enquiry at Woolwich Arsenal about the deterioration in the rockets, the explanation was forthcoming that the rockets had been made for forty years by a man who died without passing on his skill.

The Services had for some time been using a cordite rocket so the Coastguard took their problem to a committee of experts at Fort Halstead near Sevenoaks, Kent. They were delighted to be asked to design a rocket for saving life after spending the war years designing death dealing rockets.

It was decided that a three-inch cordite-filled rocket already in production would probably suit the needs of the coastguard if it was modified. The speed of flight of this rocket was much greater than the Boxer and unless it could be slowed down it would carry away the rocket lines. A suitable projector was also needed.

Trials were carried out on the Crumbles near Eastbourne, and in the early attempts the rockets did carry away many rocket lines and travelled up to one thousand yards with pieces of line attached. A length of hawser was fixed between the rocket and the rocket line to take up the snatch on firing and to steady the rocket in flight.

When the trials were completed the Life-saving Apparatus

Companies were trained in the new drill procedure needed, and within days of the rescue rocket coming into use on the Northumberland coast it was instrumental in getting a line aboard a vessel aground near Berwick upon Tweed, in weather conditions which would have been beyond the power of the old Boxer rocket.

7
Public Opinion to the Rescue

By the turn of the century there were indications that the cost of the Coastguard Service was producing the now familiar rumblings that preceded yet another reorganization.

Letters and minutes were circulating in the Admiralty, and these were followed by the first obvious signs. The coastguard ships were withdrawn from their stations round the coast and, as Admiral Ernest Rice, commanding Coastguard and Reserves put it: 'It became necessary to reorganize the Coastguard Service in 1903'.

The districts were rearranged and the coast of England divided into three; Ireland into two, and the whole of Scotland into one. Each was under command of a Captain. The district headquarters were located at Harwich, Southampton, Liverpool, Queenstown, Kingstown and Edinburgh.

The Rear-Admiral Commanding on the coast of Ireland was appointed deputy to the Admiral Commanding Coastguard and Reserves in order to supervise the service in Ireland.

The office of the Admiral Commanding Coastguard and Reserves was reconstituted on 1st April 1904 with an entirely naval instead of joint naval and civilian staff. An Engineer Captain and a commander for gunnery were added to the staff, with an Engineer Captain and a Lieutenant R.N.R. for temporary employment on recruiting duties.

The Customs, ever watchful for changes that might affect revenue protection, set up a Departmental Committee in 1906 to review the coastguard service, but while this was going on the Admiralty was allowing the service to run down.

The Committee learned that the peacetime establishment of the coastguard was thirty inspecting commanders; thirty-nine inspecting lieutenants; two hundred and fifty-four chief officers, and a total strength of 4,172 officers and men in the six districts. These contained eight-two divisions and 700 stations.

The cost to the Admiralty was estimated to be half a million pounds a year.

The Admiralty reminded the committee that the Coastguard was transferred from Customs to the Admiralty under the 1856 Coastguard Service Act which made the duties partly naval and partly civil. They considered that the naval requirements would be met by the retention of about 170 War Signal and Wireless Telegraphy Stations, crewed by about 700 officers and men. This would leave 3,400 officers and men, and, 530 stations to be dealt with, as they put it.

The civil duties were enumerated in three main categories, Revenue Protection; Non-revenue work in aid of Customs, and, Work on behalf of other Government Departments and public bodies. Revenue Protection: The coastguard was required to visit frequently creeks and byplaces where it was probable small craft might be concealed for smuggling purposes. They were held responsible for any smuggling transaction that might take place within the limits of their station or for the escape of any smugglers if due to negligence, want of courage or other misconduct.

Commanding officers of cruisers whether specially employed on the fisheries or elsewhere were required to protect the revenue. This was now confined to seizing Coopers – floating tobacco and grog shops – if found within the three mile limit and watching these craft for communication with fishing boats outside territorial waters.

Non-revenue Work: Enforcement of the Public Health regulations on ships arriving from abroad; collecting shipping statistics; registering, lettering and numbering of British sea-fishing boats; collecting Light dues; assisting Collectors of Customs as Receivers of Wreck for salvage, custody and disposal of wrecked goods.

Work for Other Government Departments and public bodies:

The custody and working of life-saving apparatus issued by the Board of Trade; duties in connection with saving of life; assisting in manning the lifeboat, although this was voluntary; reporting to Board of Trade information on wrecks and casualties, encroachments on foreshores, shifting of buoys and irregularities of lights. Reporting wrecks and casualties to Lloyd's; working

95

cautionary or storm warning signals at certain stations for the Meteorological Office; looking out for signals from lighthouses and lightships; working the Coast Communication telegraph and telephones; collecting sea-fishing statistics for the Board of Agriculture and Fisheries; work for other institutions and harbour boards.

The Admiralty thought that the arrangements made when the coastguard was transferred to the Admiralty might be considerably modified. A large proportion of the coast of the United Kingdom was still patrolled nightly by the coastguard, but looking to the increase in population and the number of towns and villages round the coast, the development of telegraphic communication and the great reduction in the inducements to smuggle, this service seemed to be no longer required.

The Committee agreed that the Customs requirements could be efficiently and more economically protected by a force under the control of the Customs. 'At the same time we consider that the paucity of detections by the Coastguard of smuggling is not evidence that a coastguard is unnecessary. All inlets, creaks and shores which are accessible to boats should be regarded as possible centres of smuggling, and some system of guard or watch maintained . . . there is neither evidence or experience to justify the withdrawal of the Coastguard from any point on the coast which would be unattended by danger to the revenue'.

Pointing out that under Article 401 of the Coastguard Instructions, each night patrol was authorized to carry a loaded pistol if the station officer thought it desirable, the committee was of the opinion that if Customs officers carried out the patrols it would be neither necessary nor expedient that they should be empowered to carry arms.

Life-saving apparatus duties performed on behalf of the Board of Trade formed an important part of the work of the Coastguard but, on 18th June 1905 the Admiralty wrote to Customs: 'Certain other duties in connection with life-saving and wrecks, under the Board of Trade, have been undertaken by the Coastguard but these, however valuable, do not constitute a *raison d'être* for the Coastguard, and it is quite feasible to make adequate local arrangements for carrying out these services'.

In the same letter the Admiralty recommended the closure of 144 coastguard stations. 'It is now considered that about 170

Lowestoft Coastguard Rescue Company saved ten-man crew of Trawler *Granada* ashore near Hopton, Suffolk, January 9th, 1970 (See chapter thirteen)

Crewman helped ashore from Trawler *Grenada* near Hopton, Suffolk, January 9th, 1970 (See chapter thirteen)

Torrey Canyon oil slic
(See chapter thirteen)

Torrey Canyon after the bombing (See chapter thirteen)

War Signal and Wireless Telegraph Stations in the United Kingdom are sufficient to give warning of the approach of an enemy's ships, and that as far as the use of the Coastguard for coast defence is concerned the remaining 530 stations and their personnel are quite unnecessary. The 170 stations mentioned must be maintained for naval purposes – for signalling use.

'The Coastguard force occupies an anomalous position in being treated as an active service force on one hand, and as merely a reserve for the Fleet on the other.

'As an active service force it is far from fulfilling modern fighting requirements in that a man's efficiency depends on his being continuously associated with highly technical duties on board ship.

'As a Reserve, though it fulfils the requirements of such a force, its cost is out of all proportion to that at which the efficient Royal Fleet Reserve can now be maintained'.

After representations were made to the Treasury by the interested parties an Interdepartmental Conference on the Coastguard was set up and reported in 1907. The report caused so much controversy that the conference was reconvened the following year.

Reviewing the relationship between the Coastguard and the Life-saving Apparatus, the conference reported that the Divisional Officer of the Coastguard was responsible for the efficiency of the rocket apparatus, and for that of the Station Officers and men who worked it whether they were coastguards or not.

At the majority of the Life-saving Apparatus Stations the apparatus was looked after and worked, with the assistance of volunteers, by the local Coastguard.

The principal duty of the Coastguard in connection with the lifeboat was to give warning to the lifeboat authorities in case of a casualty. Coastguard officers were allowed to serve on local lifeboat committees and coastguardsmen, with certain restrictions were allowed to form part of a lifeboat's crew, but such service was purely voluntary.

There were 299 lifeboats stationed at 260 places on the coasts of the United Kingdom and Channel Islands, and at 203 there were Coastguard Stations or detachments.

It was the conference proposals on life-saving duties which caused a public outcry.

D

'The Coastguard at present patrol the coast nightly and therefore it is probable that wrecks or casualties would soon come to their notice, but at the same time it is only during bad weather that this patrol is likely to be of value for life-saving purposes. As the patrol is no longer considered necessary for Revenue Protection duties there is no sufficient reason to retain the services of a large number of men all the year round, merely to keep a lookout in bad weather.

'In future the watch in bad or foggy weather, with a view to lifesaving would be: where there are naval stations by naval staff; where Customs staff have charge of Life-saving Apparatus'.

The Report included an Appendix containing extracts from Coastguard Instructions on service with lifeboats.

Officers who desired to serve in their private capacity as members of local committees and found it consistent with their duties were allowed to do so.

The post of Coxswain or Second Coxswain of a lifeboat could be held by any Chief Boatman or other man of the Coastguard, and the crews of stations were allowed to form part of a lifeboat's crew if sanctioned by the Station Officer, but it was laid down that was not intended that any of the coastguard force should be diverted from their special duties when a lifeboat's crew could be made up from the neighbouring population's seafarers and fishermen.

Coastguardsmen working the Life-saving Apparatus were not to be employed on lifeboat duties unless there were local circumstances allowing an exception to be made.

'On no account are men to be ordered on lifeboat service, and officers are to use their own judgement in allowing men under their orders to volunteer on an emergency, bearing in mind that the saving of life is of the first consideration.

'Should any man of the Coastguard lose his life while engaged on this service, his widow may be granted a pension, and his children allowances out of the funds of Greenwich Hospital'.

In an attempt to find new duties to justify the retention of the Coastguard a proposal was made that the service should take over the lifeboats. The Conference dismissed the suggestion by quoting an extract from the Report of the Select Committee of the House of Commons on the Royal National Lifeboat Institution of 1897.

'Suggestions have been made that the lifeboats should no longer be manned as at present by the fishermen and beachmen of the stations, but either by a permanent crew maintained expressly for the purpose or by the Coastguard.

'The expense of maintaining a permanent crew as compared with the present system would be so great as to be prohibitory.

'The objections to employing the Coastguard are overwhelming. The Coastguard is not sufficient in numbers. The Coastguard Stations, moreover, being selected with a view to prohibit smuggling are often not to be found where a lifeboat is most needed. The coastguardsmen are not necessarily good boatmen, and some of them have had no training as such; and in any case they are likely to be inferior in the local knowledge which gives to the beachmen and fishermen such skill in overcoming the difficulties of local currents, shoals and rocks.

'Moreover, the Coastguard being men of the first Naval Reserve are withdrawn at least once a year for naval service.

'Your Committee see no ground for recommending that the Lifeboat Service should be taken over by the State, so long as it is maintained as efficiently and successfully as at present by public benevolence.

'Your Committee consider that there are many advantages in committing the control of this service, as now, to a voluntary association of honourable men, who have, in many cases, devoted years of their lives without pay or remuneration of any sort to the cause of life-saving, relying for funds on the benificence of the people of these Kingdoms, and for crews to man the boats, on the unfailing courage and devotion of the maritime population'.

Public opinion resented the proposed reduction of the Coastguard and the abandonment of life-saving by the service. Letters were written to newspapers and a campaign was mounted to save the Coastguard.

This led to an undertaking by the Admiralty. Mr Edmund Robertson speaking on the Navy Estimates on 10th March 1908 declared: 'As to the question of the Coastguard, I am not surprised at the interest excited on both sides of the House. The proposals for the abolition of the Coastguard have been considered by an Interdepartmental Committee. The Admiralty however have undertaken to consider the question for themselves *de novo*. I have been asked whether those parts of the

99

coasts requiring to be watched for life-saving purposes will continue to be watched by H.M. Coastguard. To that I can give an answer in the affirmative. Second question, will the Coastguard be maintained wherever they assist in any material degree in manning and launching lifeboats? The answer is "yes" '.

The Interdepartmental Conference met again and recommended that life-saving should continue to be voluntary and that any responsibility that should devolve on a Government Department should devolve on the Board of Trade. The Coastguard and Customs helping as before when practicable.

The scheme was then laid before the Treasury who, mindful of public opinion, objected on the ground that miscellaneous duties carried out by the Coastguard would best be done by men under service discipline, and under one Department. They also refused to accept the principle that naval expenditure should be restricted to combatant functions, or that appropriations in aid should be given for services rendered to other Departments by the Admiralty. The Admiralty then dropped the matter, restricted the Coastguard to 3,100 officers and men and made no additions merely for coast-watching.

The attitude of the Admiralty to the Coastguard can be judged from the report of Admiral Sir Reginald Henderson, K.G.B., on giving up the command of the Coastguard and Naval Reserves at the end of 1909.

'The policy which has guided me during my command from 1905-09 has been based as far as practicable on the two important considerations laid down in their Lordships' "Statement of Admiralty Policy, 1905."

'1. The whole object of the Navy Estimates is to secure the fighting efficiency of the Fleet and its instant readiness for war.

'2. The money asked for the Navy should be the least possible compatible with the above necessities.

'I have recognized that so long as the Admiralty are responsible for revenue protection ashore and afloat, and for the protection of the fisheries on the high seas, and to some extent for the life-saving services on the coasts, it is not practicable to carry out to its logical conclusion the policy contained in those two considerations. I have, however, endeavoured to reduce the expenditure on non-naval services as much as possible, both as regards personnel and material, with a view that such reduction in each case would result in a corresponding addition to the resources in men and money of the Fleet'.

In an accompanying table the Admiral showed a saving of £124,000 by reducing the Coastguard strength from 4,135 to 3,100. This also allowed an increase of 1,035 ratings for the fleet.

An additional 150 wireless telegraph operators were provided from the Coastguard for the Shore Wireless Telegraph Stations.

Ships on coastguard duties, which consisted in the main of conveying coastguardsmen and their families and belongings from one station to another, and distributing stores, were withdrawn. This work, it was stated could be done with more economy and with greater comfort to the men and their families, by land.

The total number of coastguardsmen on shore duties on 1st January 1905 was 4,135. Entry of men from the Fleet continued up to the beginning of 1906 when entries were suspended. The strength then decreased by normal wastage to 3,085 by 1911.

The 3,100 were six District Captains, twenty-four Commanders, thirty-six Lieutenants; sixteen Divisional Chief Officers, 171 Chief Officers, 313 Chief Boatmen-in-charge, 335 Chief Boatmen, 1,342 Commissioned Boatmen and 800 Boatmen.

The Admiral explained the policy pursued for reducing the Coastguard in four stages between 1905-09.

1905-07 the stations and detachments at which extensive repairs were required or new buildings needed, and whose duties did not justify such expenditure from the naval point of view were closed and a corresponding reduction of personnel effected.

1907-08 the closing of stations was suspended on 31st March 1907 pending consideration of the Report of the Interdepartmental Conference on the Coastguard.

The normal reduction of personnel continued during this period and in consequence many stations became short of men.

The Admiral who presided at the Conference which was

attended by representatives of the Admiralty, Board of Trade, Board of Customs, Scottish Office and Irish Office, listed the main recommendations:

The system of dual control was considered unsatisfactory by the Admiralty and the Board of Customs as it led to friction and inefficiency. The maintenance of two separate forces for similar duties entailed the maintenance of two separate supervising staffs. They therefore considered it desirable in the interests of economy and efficiency of revenue protection that the system of dual control should end, and that the whole duty of collection, management and protection of the revenue should be under control of the Board of Customs.

The strength of the Coastguard was in excess of all requirements on shore, and there was not sufficient justification for the employment of a permanent force solely for life-saving work.

The third stage from 1908-09. The Conference report showed that there were nearly 100 stations and detachments whose duties naval or non-naval did not justify their maintenance.

'On 21st March 1908 the Board authorized me to close such redundant stations at which neither life-saving apparatus was supplied nor lifeboat stationed, and, eighty-four stations and detachments with a total complement of 452 were closed between May 1908 and April 1909'.

The personnel from these stations were used to fill vacancies at others which had been allowed to run down.

The fourth stage – 1909. In view of the policy of assistance by the Coastguard to the life-saving services no more stations or detachments were closed but the normal reduction of personnel continued and in consequence it was necessary to reduce the complements of the existing stations.

The Treasury having refused to adopt the recommendations of the Coastguard Conference, the Admiralty directed Admiral Henderson to draw up a scheme to reorganize the Service based on the Conference report, except that the men would remain in the Coastguard instead of being transferred to the Board of Customs.

Commenting on the unfavourable reaction to the report the Admiral had this to say: 'In regard to certain discussions in the

House of Commons, and public opinion generally, the services of the Coastguard in regard to life-saving have frequently been allowed to completely overshadow the actual duties for which the Coastguard is maintained, and while it is obvious that the more men there are stationed to watch the coasts the less likelihood there is of wrecks and marine casualties being unnoticed, it is not apparent why the Admiralty should maintain a permanent force for purely life-saving purposes, especially as the Conference had stated that there was not sufficient justification for any permanent force for this work.

'It seems desirable, however, that this issue should be kept clearly defined as the valuable assistance hitherto rendered by the Coastguard to the life-saving services has led up to the general view of the public that the Coastguard is provided solely for these purposes; it should also be noted that in war or in an emergency three-quarters of the personnel would be required for service with the Fleet'.

The Admiral referred in his report to the Coastguard work in protection of the revenue and pointed out that they had not had to deal with any attempts at large-scale smuggling, and except for about a dozen cases of minor smuggling of small quantities of tobacco or liquor their preventive duties had been of a purely passive nature but he thought that their presence acted as a deterrent.

All men of the non-naval section of the Coastguard, if under fifty years old, embarked biennially for twenty-eight days in the Home Fleet during manoeuvres, as part of the complement of the 3rd and 4th Divisions of the Fleet. They were also continuously instructed in the use of small arms and in signalling and telegraphy.

In 1909 there were 109 Visual Signal Stations manned in peace and thirty-one additional which would be manned in war. Visual signalling was also carried out at eleven of the Wireless Telegraph Stations. The Admiral commented that it was the efficiency of the War Signal Stations on which the system of distribution of intelligence entirely depended.

The men were required to reach a standard of eighteen to twenty words a minute with the semaphore and ten words a minute with the flashing light. At each War Signal Station there was at least one man able to read sixty words or more in five

103

minutes. The acetylene lamps used for flashing signals were replaced by oil lamps which allowed signals to be exchanged at twelve miles range.

There was a great advance in the efficiency of the Shore Naval Telegraph Stations in five years. In December, 1904 there were seven, each with five qualified W/T operators, and with a maximum range of seventy-five miles. By 1909 there were two high-powered stations with a range of 1,000 miles; four medium stations with a range of 500 miles, six low-powered stations with 200 miles range and four with 100 miles range, all worked by Coastguards for the Navy.

The Coastguard also manned two small powered stations for the army in the Channel Islands, and four others for the G.P.O

The run-down of the Coastguard Service alarmed the Board of Trade because it showed up the inadequacy of the coast-watching arrangements, and the Board proposed to the Treasury a scheme for establishing permanently employed coast-watchers at certain places. The Treasury suggested the watchers should be part-time, but the Board of Trade thought that part-time men would not give efficient watch.

The Board of Trade then asked the Admiralty to consider establishing stations at certain places, and that the Admiralty should so man the Coastguard Stations that, except in war, constant watch could always be kept in bad weather. They also suggested that the Admiralty should provide Coastguard Stations where required for coast-watching.

As an alternative scheme they suggested that the Board of Trade should take over all Coastguard Stations except War Signal and Port War Signal Stations, and staff them with naval pensioners, not to be withdrawn without Board of Trade sanction. The pensioners would carry out Customs duties.

The Admiralty replied that as every trained man would be wanted for service with the Fleet during peace and on mobilization they could not re-establish coastguard stations that had been closed, or open new stations not required for naval service, but they gave an assurance that, as before, the Coastguard would help coast-watching as much as they could.

The war came before any agreement was reached. By this time the Board of Trade had built some huts in readiness for coast-watching. The last letter before the war from the Admiralty to the Board of Trade enquired whether if certain stations were opened purely for coast-watching, the Board would obtain Treasury sanction to pay the cost.

8
The Coastguard Goes to War

A slow decline into oblivion may have been the Admiralty's plan for the Coastguard Service, but the air of decay and obsolescence which pervaded the structure surprisingly stopped short of the morale of the men.

Perhaps it was their traditional role of 'Cinderella' of the services which enabled them to shrug off the feeling of impending doom, and, though short of manpower at many stations and with station buildings falling into disrepair, the men trained hard for the war that loomed. The state of the stations can be judged from a Minute of the Director of Works at the Admiralty, dated 1912:

'First Lord gave me verbal instructions last week, when he was considering Draft Vote 1912-1913, that he would not provide money for building any new Coastguard Stations which are not required for war purposes.

'We have a considerable number of Coastguard Stations where accommodation is distinctly bad – so bad that it could not be defended if questions were raised about Government servants being housed in such premises'.

In the previous year the ranks of the Coastguard were changed to bring them closer to the navy titles. Chief Officers and Boatmen remained unchanged, but the rank of Chief Petty Officer replaced that of the Chief Boatman, and Commissioned Boatmen became Leading Boatmen. The uniform was changed to that worn by Chief Petty Officers of the navy.

Efforts were already being made in 1912 to work-up the Coastguard to a high state of war readiness, and the Admiral Commanding Coastguard and Reserves decided it was most important that coastguard ratings, particularly the crews of Wireless Telegraph Stations and War Signal Stations should be capable of defending themselves against attack.

He proposed that to encourage the men to become proficient in pistol firing there should be a small grant of prize-money. Calculated at 3d per head of the personnel this would provide £37 10s 0d. There would be one prize of 30/- for the best shot in the Coastguard for the year; one prize of 15/- for the best shot in each district; and other prizes of 10/- and 5/-. After some correspondence the idea was approved and each man was allocated one hundred rounds of ammunition per year for target practice.

War preparations were speeded up when Vice-Admiral Arthur M. Farquhar, C.V.O. took over as Admiral Commanding Coastguard and Reserves in 1913. The emphasis was placed on the naval role of the Coastguard and this took precedence over all other work.

The training, discipline and efficiency of the service brought surprised congratulations from the Navy after the order to mobilize came in 1914.

The Coastguard war plan swung smoothly into action, and most of the Station crews had their kits packed and were ready to entrain for the naval depots within an hour of the mobilization telegram being received. Many of the station officers were on leave at the time and senior ratings were in charge of stations. These men had the responsibility of seeing the plan set in motion.

The smaller stations were entirely abandoned as the crews went to their battle headquarters, but the vacuum was filled by the army who took over the buildings and set up coast patrols. The wife of the Station Officer at each abandoned station was allowed to stay on, if she wished, to take naval calls on the Coast Communications Telephone. For this she was paid 5/- a week.

The army took over the watch-house and telephone, but as the navy still had a woman representing them at the station, the coastguard routine was maintained with official inspections by the District Captain from time to time.

At the stations which were kept open with reduced crews, the army took over many of the coast patrols, and the coastguardsmen were officially under their orders, but as the soldiers were inexperienced in ship spotting and lacked local knowledge, they relied on the coastguards for advice.

Shortage of manpower prevented efficient coast and beach patrols from being kept and civilians were called in to help.

Many of them were local Boy Scouts who did excellent work and were quick to learn from the coastguardsmen.

One of them, still an Auxiliary Coastguard fifty years later, Mr I. T. King of Winterton-on-Sea recalled that early in 1918 at the age of fifteen he was offered a job as a Coastwatching Scout attached to the Coastguard Service as an Auxiliary. The Coastguard of Winterton had been gradually reduced by calls to active service to one petty officer and two ratings, augmented by one aged civilian auxiliary and four lively youths.

The duties were to man the lookout with a Coastguard for twenty-four hours. Off-watch duties included keeping the station clean and tidy, polishing up the Life-saving Apparatus cart and equipment, scrubbing out the quarters daily, cleaning the rifles, and taking messages to the Senior Naval Officer at Gorleston, a twenty minute cycle ride away. Occasionally one of the boys was sent to the lighthouse with instructions for the light to be lit when a convoy was due to pass in the night. Mr King was paid 13/- a week and had uniform provided free of charge, but 10/- was deducted for meals which were provided by the petty officer's wife. The boys slept in an old coastguard look out and boathouse on the sand dues.

Within a short time of the outbreak of war, the Coastguard, with the exception of those over age and the officers and men required for the War Signal Stations, were embarked in ships of the navy for service at sea, the role for which the service had been prepared since 1856. It was a highly successful operation and enabled many ships to go to sea which would have been held up in port until crews could be recruited.

But the speed and efficiency of the Coastguard which got the ships to sea meant that vessels which were no match for the modern German Imperial Fleet perished gloriously in action, taking many coastguardsmen to their deaths. Some of the first coastguard casualties were in three cruisers sunk near the mouth of the Thames on 20th September 1914. The action was later described by Admiral Sir Dudley de Chair as a regrettable accident.

'The sinking of three of the first class cruisers of the Cressy class by a single submarine, in the Deep Fourteens off the mouth of the Thames, was really due to unfortunate orders issued by the Admiralty, and, not allowing Admirals in command of squadrons a free hand in the handling of their ships.

'Apparently the Admirals in command had represented urgently how futile it was for their ships to patrol at slow speed and in close order when in submarine waters, but no notice was taken. The result was that Lieutenant-Commander Wennigen in *U9*, working by himself, had a sitting shot at *Cressy* which, being hit below the waterline, filled and turned over sinking with the majority of her officers and men.

'*Aboukir* went to her assistance and was immediately sunk by another torpedo, and then the third large cruiser *Hogue* steamed into the picture to rescue those in the water and was also sunk. Thus the whole squadron succumbed to a single submarine.

'1,400 officers and men were lost, and sixty officers and seventy-seven men saved.

'The Tenth Cruiser Squadron on patrol of Scapa on 15th October 1914 was attacked by submarines and H.M.S. *Hawke* sunk with the loss of 500 men. One of the survivors reported that she was hit by a torpedo and capsized within fifteen minutes.

'Early in January 1915 H.M.S. *Formidable* a battleship of Admiral Lewis Bayly's squadron was torpedoed in the English Channel close off the Start, with great loss of life. All these disasters swelled the Coastguard Roll of Honour'.

Corbett in *History of the Great War: Naval Operations* commented on the loss of the cruisers 'to give the last touch of bitterness the old cruisers, being amongst the latest to mobilize, were manned mainly by R.N. reserve ratings, most of whom were married men with families, yet in spite of the rawness of the crews, and the appalling nature of the disaster, by every testimony the discipline displayed was admirable and the conduct of the men beyond all praise, both before and after the ships went down.

'As for the ships themselves their loss was a small matter. They were ill-adapted for naval warfare in its recent developments and were obsolescent. But the crews, seeing how devotedly they had come forward from their civilian occupations at the country's call, were a national loss to be lamented'.

It was soon realized that the men of the Coastguard were needed on the coasts more urgently under wartime conditions than in peace. They were, therefore, disembarked and sent back

109

to the Coastguard Stations to ensure that the coasts were adequately watched against the landing of enemy agents and attack by enemy ships, and, to make efficient arrangements for the saving of life.

The depleted crews were brought up to strength with auxiliary coastguardsmen. The duties expanded in wartime and included the dangerous job of defusing sea-mines washed ashore.

Before the war started little training had been given in this work in the navy, and none at all to the Coastguard. Early in the war coastguardsmen were sent to special courses at Navy Torpedo Schools where the art of rendering mines harmless was taught using German mines which had been washed ashore. The coastguards soon became the most knowledgeable people on the subject. After training the mine experts were posted to Coastguard Stations twenty miles apart. They were excused ordinary coastguard duties but were on call at all times.

The Admiralty instruction was that they must use the utmost dispatch in proceeding to the spot where a mine was ashore, and, with the tools provided, to make the mine safe. They then went back to their station to be ready for the next call leaving the mine to be removed by the crew of a coastguard cutter.

The enemy mines at that time had as detonators short lead horns attached to the body of the mine. These contained a glass tube of acid which, when broken, soaked onto the detonating charge. The Coastguard on mine watch would carefully remove the horns but to do this he would often have to dig the mine out of the soft sand. He could call on other coastguardsmen to help him uncover the mine, but when this was done they were ordered to retreat five hundred yards while the horns were disconnected.

One story told by Frank Bowen, in his book published in the 1920s, is of a coastguard who was hurriedly sent for by a fishing port where a mine had been landed by a trawler which had picked it up in the fishing nets. When he arrived he found that the horns had been broken off. He expressed surprise but the old fisherman just changed his pipe to the other side of his mouth and remarked, 'Well, Sir, we heard that those were the dangerous parts so we just broke them off with a boat-hook'.

Five soldiers were blown to pieces on the Kent coast when they ignored warnings from a coastguard not to touch a mine which could only be removed from an awkward position with a rope. The coastguard went back to his station to fetch the equipment but was stopped by an army officer who wanted to ask him some questions. As he approached the beach but was still several hundred yards away, the mine went off.

The older men of the service who had been trained in the days of sail found their services in great demand when anti-submarine nets were required to protect the entrances to harbours. These men, who were experts in the splicing of ropes, were sent to navy dockyards and supervised the work of making the nets.

The War Signal Stations and Wireless Telegraphy Stations became the nerve centres of naval intelligence. Their crews of coastguardsmen were kept at full strength, and some had extra men posted to them to deal with the huge number of messages which flowed in. All naval ships communicated with the Admiralty through the stations when close enough to the shore to give visual signals, and all merchant ships passing the stations were logged and their owners informed of their progress.

The importance of the Wireless Telegraphy Stations increased as more ships were fitted with the necessary equipment. These stations had already reached a high standard of efficiency due to the interest taken before the war by the Coastguard.

By 1913 regular exercises simulating wartime conditions were being carried out.

In addition to their normal wireless work the stations had other duties added as the war progressed. With the advent of the Zeppelin raids the Wireless Telegraphy Station at Sheerness controlled the London air defence stations for more than two years. When the public demanded air raid warnings it was to the Coastguard that the authorities turned. A naval officer pointed out that the coastguard held stocks of maroons for calling out the lifeboat. These stocks were sent to London and became the first public air raid warning system.

The Port Signal Stations were also manned by the coastguard and the officer in charge, usually a former R.N. Lieutenant, was responsible for identifying all vessels entering and leaving port, and was in charge of the signals given for opening and closing the defence boom.

After many years experience at sea and in the Coastguard the officers and men of the service were expert in the identifica-

III

tion of every type of vessel, and this proved invaluable as no
other service had made a study of the art.

In addition to their normal patrol work the coastguardsmen
were expected to assist the police and army to round up escaped
prisoners-of-war and Frank Bowen records one such incident:
During the war the great military depot of Richborough on the
Kent coast was manned very largely by German prisoners, and
one night three of them escaped.

Some three hundred soldiers were immediately aroused from
their quarters and sent out in every direction to hunt for the
Germans. The hunt lasted for twenty-four hours without finding
any trace of them, but about two o'clock in the morning of the
second night the Coastguard rating who was patrolling the coast
from No. 2 Battery Station, a relic of the Napoleonic wars, saw
something moving near the Coastguard boat which was drawn
up on the beach.

He immediately approached as stealthily as he could and
before he was detected he saw three men getting the cover off the
boat which they evidently intended to launch in the hope of getting away.

He dashed up, covered them with his revolver and ordered
them to put their hands up. Two of them obeyed but the third
man took to his heels and ran off into the darkness. The coastguard very wisely decided that two birds in the hand were
very much more worth his while than one in the desolate sandhills round the station and marched his prisoners off to the
military headquarters.

As soon as he had handed them over he returned to the search
and had scoured the beach for some distance before he came
across a large pile of seaweed similar to a hundred others. However, he was taking no chances so he took a running kick at it
and was immediately rewarded by a loud grunt. As a matter of
fact he had kicked his quarry fairly in the stomach and had
knocked all the wind out of him. Before he could make off he
found himself covered by the Coastguard's revolver and politely
requested to come along and join his two friends.

The war had intervened in the discussions on the role of the
Coastguard, and had, incidentally, proved that as a Naval Reserve
the men had given magnificent and heroic service, but it also
showed that the 1906 Committee recommendations were right.

The dual role was incompatible. The mobilization of the Coastguard which enabled ships to be manned and at sea within a few days, left the coasts completely unguarded.

By landing the Coastguard and returning the men to their Stations meant that the role of the Fleet Reserve was impossible to fulfil.

In 1919 the Admiralty reorganized the Force and again started discussions about the future of the service.

The Coastguard New Force, as it was called, was organized on a naval pensioner basis, and, in a Memorandum, the Naval Law Branch of the Admiralty described the change. 'It is perhaps the case that, in founding the new Coastguard Force, discipline was a little overlooked, and a quasi-civilian force was created incorporating a new master-and-servant feature of a month's notice. The system of discipline, proposed by the Admiral Commanding Reserves, for the new force was a simple one of very few punishments for minor offences, but a couple of reprimands for minor offences was to entail discharge under the terms of the agreement.

'It was hoped that this system being thoroughly understood would work satisfactorily, and the Coastguard New Force would be a *Corps d'Elite*. It seems doubtful on consideration whether this system will work satisfactorily and whether we are not forced to fall back on a system of punishments something like that existing for the Navy generally or the Coastguard Old Force.'

The new form of agreement did not alter the amenability of the new force to the Naval Discipline Act by way of the Coastguard Act, just as in the case of the old force. The question of 'discharge by purchase' in the Coastguard is raised. The maintenance of the Coastguard is an expensive matter and voluntary discharge must be put at a high price. It is then realized that there will be a temptation to undergo two mild reprimands and leave the force for nothing at a month's notice rather than by paying £40–£50 for discharge by purchase.

It was proposed that the system of discipline for the new force should be laid down that officers and men entered in or transferred to the new force were, for disciplinary purposes, subject to the Naval Discipline Act and the Laws and Customs of the Navy, with a new punishment of fines for general offences other than drunkenness and improper absence from duty, for men of

Petty Officer and Leading Seaman ranks. Not exceeding thirty days' pay for any offence or offences punished at the time.

If the fine exceeded seven days' pay it was to be with approval of the Captain of the area, but the question of fines was disputed by Admiral Commanding Reserves de Chair who thought that punishments for men of the new force should be reduced to a minimum compatible with effective discipline, an extensive list of petty punishments being undesirable in the case of selected ratings of very good character, with twenty-two years' service discipline behind them.

He suggested that fines for old and new forces should be abolished and reprimands instituted with the ulterior object of reducing habitual minor offences to a minimum, by holding over the men the fear of discharge from the Coastguard under the terms of their agreement should they prove a continual nuisance to the Coastguard Service in general, without actually committing an offence serious enough to warrant discharge for misconduct.

His opinion prevailed and the only offences for which men could be fined were improper absence and unfitness for duty through drink, as laid down in King's Regulations.

On discharge from the Coastguard before completion of engagement, New Force ratings were paid the gratuity they had earned. Removal expenses were paid by the Crown and they were allowed to keep their kit, provided that all buttons and badges were removed. They were also given twenty-eight days' pay in lieu of notice.

If they were dismissed from the Coastguard, the new force men forfeited their gratuity, had to pay for their removal, lost the twenty-eight days' pay in lieu of notice, and had to pay for their kit.

Within eighteen months of the end of the war a Naval Staff Conference was convened to report on the Coastguard and the Wireless Stations. While it was sitting a memorandum was circulated to senior Coastguard officers pointing out that it became the custom for senior naval officers around the coast to perform many duties during the war which had previously been carried out by other authorities. 'This custom should now cease and pre-war arrangements should be reverted to, so that the duties performed by the naval coast organization other than its normal coastguard duties may be restricted to those which can only be carried out by a naval authority'.

The Staff Conference reported that their examination of the distribution of the Coastguard Stations showed that in the past it was influenced to a great extent by the urgent need to prevent smuggling from the Continent. On the south-east coast the stations were therefore very close together and the further they were from that area the more widely separated they became. This unequal distribution did not lend itself to future naval requirements.

Soon after the declaration of war the existing look-out and watching system was found to be inadequate. The submarine and aerial menace together with the threat of invasion necessitated a particular close watch being kept on the east and south-east coasts, those very coasts which in the past had been specially equipped against the smuggler. As the war progressed and other parts of the coasts came within the radius of hostile action this watching system was extended until it was in operation almost all round the coasts of the British Isles.

It absorbed a considerable personnel including coastguardsmen recalled from the Fleet, R.N.V.R., Boy Scouts and civilians. To house these and provide telephone and headquarters facilities the majority of the Coastguard Stations were used.

The system was not uniformly efficient because of varying conditions and resources on the different parts of the coast.

On the south and east coasts of England the efficiency was high because there was generally a numerous naval personnel to assist the untrained civilian watchers; where there was not, reports could be checked by the trained personnel of the War Signal Station which was in telephonic communication with the Coastguard Stations. On the west coast of Scotland the system did not work satisfactorily because there were very few trained personnel, the stations were widely scattered and there was no continuous telephone circuit. The civilian watchers were not in all cases whole-timers but did the work while carrying on their farming etc.

The Conference considered that coast-watching would be necessary in the future and should be provided for on any coast where it was possible that an enemy could operate or make use of a harbour for refuge. It was very important that the personnel should be composed of a large percentage of naval men with many years experience of the sea. These men should have peace-time experience of any stretch of the coast on which they might be employed in war.

The coast-watching organization for any coast should be worked out locally in detail so that it could be brought into operation immediately on mobilization.

While these plans for the future of the Coastguard were being considered it was already discernible that the Navy was losing interest in the service as it was no longer a naval reserve.

9
The Coastguard has its 'Troubles'

The return of peace and the upheaval of the latest re-organization had hardly been absorbed when the Coastguard in Ireland found themselves once again in the firing line, facing the bombs and bullets of 'the troubles'.

The Coastguard Stations were the targets of the rebels by whom they were regarded as symbols of imperialist Britain. Although some coastguards were killed and injured, in most attacks on their Stations the rebels treated the men and their families with courtesy, and allowed them to remove their personal effects before setting fire to the buildings.

The attacks had already started when the Commander-in-Chief, Western Approaches was asked by the Admiralty for his views on the reorganization of the Coastguard Service in Ireland. Admiral Tupper replied that the state of unrest rendered it difficult to suggest what stations were or were not required.

'At present it seems quite useless to have any War Signal Stations or War Watching Stations that cannot be readily accessible from seaward for victualling and manning purposes', he reported. 'Owing to interrupted land communications such stations are easily rendered quite useless for the purpose for which they exist by ill-disposed persons cutting the land wires, and it would appear that if our system of complete coastwise communication is to be preserved in Ireland all such stations should be connected to a fortified port by underground or submarine cable.

'At present the majority of Coastguard Stations are only able to carry out in a minor degree their duties because of the uncertainty of communication, and the general hostility displayed by the inhabitants, which confines the ratings to the vicinity of their stations.

'About thirty Coastguard Stations are garrisoned by Marines; about fourteen have been destroyed; the fate of the remaining one hundred stations is uncertain until some definite policy is adopted to prevent the rebels from making further attacks'.

By October 1920 the Admiral was opposed to greatly reducing the number of Coastguard Stations in Ireland or abolishing the Coastguard Force.

He claimed that the presence of coastguardsmen on the coast, in addition to their usefulness for patrolling, customs duties and saving life, had a considerable influence on the population. He thought that pensioner coastguards were eminently more fitted for the work of a Customs force than civilians with no sea experience.

In a signal to the Admiralty he declared, 'It is from my point of view essential to have officers and men in the coast watching service, principal ports and signal stations who understand the Navy and have been accustomed to work with it. And who also are in close touch with and understand the natives.

'Although the number of Coastguard Stations attacked since the present rebellion began has been considerable, the general feeling of the coastline population is not hostile to the Coast-guard. In a few localities this statement must be modified, but it is believed that the attacks on the Stations generally speaking have been organized and ordered by the Central Committee of the Irish Republican Brotherhood and carried out by men the majority of whom have come from a distance and who have coerced a few of the local men into joining them in these raids.

'When the present rebellion has subsided, I submit that it would be a sound policy to increase the Coastguard Force in Ireland, establishing in the south-west, west and north-west of the country men, and their families, who have had more experience of civilized life than obtains in those localities normally. This would have the effect of civilizing the neighbourhood'.

The Irish Coastguard records on the attacks against their stations gives a dramatic insight into the trials and tribulations of the service at that time.

Coastguard Station, BALLINAGALL, 13th May 1920.

At midnight last night the watchman, after calling out his relief and whilst waiting to be relieved, was held up by about thirty armed, masked men who covered him with rifles and ordered him to put up his hands and surrender. He had no opportunity of firing but managed to drop his pistol in the bushes. The men made him prisoner and marched him to the watchroom. There they demanded that he open it, and when he said he could not, they broke the door open with crowbars. In the rush which followed the watchman escaped and made his way to the upper watchroom through the back door of his house and the communicating doors.

With the help of the Petty Officer he managed to secure the door with the bolt inside. The raiders attacked again firing rifles, smashing windows and called on the Coastguard to surrender, but we continued to defend the watchroom until 2 a.m. when the raiders retired. We endeavoured to attract police with rockets and signal lamps as the telephone wires were cut.

The morning man on coming to relieve was covered by five or six men with rifles who emerged from the bushes in front of the cottages and ordered him to put his hands up. He managed to drop his pistol and kicked it backwards. He was made prisoner.

The forenoon watchman hearing shots got up and, not being able to get through the communicating doors, because of the bolt being left on in the house next door, went out and was made prisoner until the raiders retired. The defence of the watchroom was successful and all arms and ammunition intact.

A fortnight later the C-in-C Western Approaches informed the Admiralty that an attack had been made on the Coastguard Station at Brandon Quay.

'These attacks appear to point to an altered attitude of Sinn Fein towards the Navy. These cases are really on a parallel with the attacks on the police barracks and the burning of government offices and property.

'It is understood there are some 157 Coastguard, War Signal and Wireless Telegraphy Stations in Ireland. The Coastguard who are issued with revolvers are engaged on patrol duty and the question of how effectively, with such outrages, is an extremely difficult one. If the Coastguard Stations themselves are put in a state of defence, by means of such expedients as increased personnel, mining, barbed wire, live wire etc., it will not provide for attacks on the Coastguards themselves when on patrol.

'It appears to be a question which must be viewed from the whole standpoint of the present situation in Ireland with which the military are intimately concerned, and it is for consideration whether the Admiralty should not officially express their view that the time has arrived when martial law should be proclaimed in Ireland'.

The next day the Admiral, Queenstown telegraphed the Admiralty reporting on an interview he had had in Dublin with civil and military heads, which had resulted in a statement that under the present circumstances the police and military forces were unable to assist all Coastguard Stations.

The G.O.C., Cork however agreed to send a small guard as a temporary measure to assist the Coastguard to hold Ballinagall and Dingle Bay Coastguard Stations.

The Admiral sent naval vessels to guard Ballinagall, Dingle Bay and Fenit Tarbert, and suggested that, as the army did not have enough men to guard the Coastguard Stations and the police were being reorganized, the only efficient method was to give each Coastguard Station ten Marines and use destroyers to visit and provision the Stations.

At midnight that night the Coastguard Station at Brandon Quay was surrounded by two hundred men, two houses were broken into and the Coastguard was called on to surrender to the Irish Republic. Three shots were fired and the Chief Officer and four coastguardsmen made prisoner. They were bound and searched and then thrown over a wall. The women and children were given time to dress and secure their valuables, and were ordered to clear out of the house. The windows were then smashed and everything saturated with petrol and tar, and set on fire. All the houses were burned out and very little furniture was saved. The raiders marched round the station and cheered.

The Chief Officer was told that the raiders were out to destroy property and his would not be the last unarmed station to be destroyed. The confidential books of the station were burned by the Coastguard and did not fall into the raiders hands. This band of rebels went on to Ballyheigue Coastguard Station at 2 a.m. where there was a complement of Chief Officer and three men. Ballyheigue was an extremely strongly built defensive station with heavy iron doors and a strong central tower.

When the raiders arrived they lit flares which were seen by the watchman who roused the others, and they rallied in the central tower. The watchman went up to the flat roof of the tower and when he saw two hundred men he suggested that they should surrender, and the Chief Officer agreed. They opened the door without destroying the confidential books and the raiders then set the building alight.

A description of a typical attack was sent by Lieutenant-Commander H. M. Hughes of H.M.S. *Urchin* to the C-in-C Western Approaches.

'The attack on the police barracks at Fenit on the night 1st-2nd June 1920 – The ship was lying alongside the pier. The following arrangements had been made for the defence of the Coastguard Station. One leading seaman and four A.B.s armed with revolvers were sent each night as reinforcements, with two Lewis-guns and two rifles for the sentries on guard outside. On any sign of trouble a rocket was to be fired as a signal to the ship.

'An armed sentry was placed fo'c'sle at night to watch the pier and coastguard station and give the alarm when the rocket was fired. His orders were to challenge and fire on anyone approaching the ship.

'A landing party of one petty officer and four men were detailed, with guns, ready to land and proceed on the first alarm. A boat was in readiness if required to land on the beach.

'The fore 4-in. gun was loaded with blank, and the aft 4-in. gun was trained on a clear space to the left of the Coastguard Station, ready to fire shell. A searchlight was worked continuously throughout the night'.

The Coastguard Station was put in a state of defence and had the windows sandbagged. Commander Hughes set the scene.

The pier was connected to the shore by a wooden viaduct sixty yards long and at the far end inshore was the railway station. Beyond that was the Customs House and beyond that again the Coastguard Station, all three on one side of the railway. A bridge crossed the railway and the village was on the other side with the police barracks at the far end about 500 yards from the Coastguard Station.

On the night of the attack it was dark and the weather thick with drizzling rain so that the searchlight was not of much use.

At 03.00 on the 2nd a rocket was seen to be fired on shore and the sentry at once gave the alarm.

A flare was observed followed by much firing and many

explosions, but, owing to the thickness of the weather, the exact nature of the attack and the course of events could not be seen from the ship.

'I immediately dispatched the landing party under Leading Seaman Hughes to the Coastguard Station and gave the gunner orders to fire a round of 4-in. blank.

'Owing to the bad visibility I decided not to fire shell but continued firing blank at intervals, which I consider had a moral effect and frightened the rebels. Another party was soon sent under orders of Sub-Lieutenant Wright, with a Lewis-gun and rifles, some Pyrenes, and a signalman. As soon as the first advance party had left the ship and were running along the pier, the inshore end of the pier burst into flames.

'It appears evident that a small party of the rebels were detailed to prevent assistance from the ship by destroying the pier, but my men arrived before they were able to complete their work, and they quickly made off along the foreshore, firing at the men as they went. There was no cover but the men lay down on the pier and returned the fire, but the rebels made good their escape in the dark under cover of the rocks. The men eventually gained the Coastguard Station as ordered.

'The house adjoining the police barracks was now in flames and the police remained in their barracks, firing on the rebels in all directions so that, in the dark and confusion, it was impossible to go to their assistance.

'I had given my men strict injunctions not to fire haphazard or without orders and to keep together. Sub-Lieutenant Wright attempted to reconnoitre with his party of men with the intention of engaging some of the rebels, but he observed that they were encircling the Coastguard Station under cover of walls at a distance, and decided to fall back for defence.

'The rebels appeared to be wonderfully well organized and kept under cover in extended order. Signals were passed by whistle which could be distinctly heard over a large area.

'Orders were also heard but could not be understood. After firing a few shots at indistinct objects, two blasts on the whistle were heard and the rebels made a sudden retreat, so quickly that they must have had cars in rear in readiness.

'At 04.00 the engagement ceased and we proceeded to the police barracks where it was difficult to persuade them to come out. The fire was by now beyond control and dangerous to approach as bombs and ammunition were exploding.

'The sergeant of police was found to be rather badly wounded and two others slightly hurt. I got them to the Coastguard Station and rendered first aid.

'All the wires were found to be cut, and all roads to Tralee thoroughly blocked, so I sent a man in plain clothes on a bicycle to endeavour to reach Tralee to inform the military and the police, and to get a doctor. He overtook a large number of men engaged in blocking the road and was sent back three times.

'At the first sign of attack I called Tralee Military Barracks by W/T but could get no reply, and it appears that no one was looking out after midnight. Had they received the signal I am convinced a patrol could have captured a large number of the rebels in their retreat'.

It was found out after the attack that the occupants of the first house across the bridge – the nearest to the Coastguard Station – had been held prisoner during the attack. There is no doubt that an attack on the Coastguard Station was intended but called off at the last minute, owing presumably to the failure to fire the pier and stop my men, and, their dislike of the 4-in. guns being fired. The rebels left three shot guns behind, and a collar and tie were found smeared with blood, so it is probable they had a casualty. None of my men was hit though all came under fire on their way to the Coastguard Station.

Lieutenant-Commander Hughes asked for more men because, out of the crew of eighteen, there were twelve available for guard at the coastguard station, working the searchlight, extra sentry duty and work on the ship. 'I am unable to land a party strong enough to round up the rebels in an attack'.

There is no record to show if the extra men were provided but, when Commander Hughes' report reached the Admiralty the C-in-C was 'requested by their Lordships to convey to Lieutenant-Commander Hughes an expression of their Lordships' satisfaction at the manner in which he carried out his duties'.

The evacuation of some Coastguard Stations which could not be defended, proved to be no simple matter. The closing of Glen Bay Station, twelve miles over the mountain road from Teelin the nearest available harbour was a case in point.

On 17th June, Malinmore Coastguard Station which was the outlying Signal hut for Glen Bay Station was burned, and the main Coastguard Station was considered to be in danger of attack. An armed party under Lieutenant C. W. V. T. S. Lepper, R.N. was landed on 19th June from H.M.S. *Serene*, to guard the Station.

Many attempts to evacuate the Station by sea were made but the coast was unsuitable for the embarkation of furniture and stores. An attempt was then made to evacuate by road on 31st July, the military having lent two large lorries with an officer and small guard of soldiers. One of the lorries sank through the road surface, and the other got into a bog some miles from Glen Bay. An armed party was landed from H.M.S. *Valkyrie* and went by car from Killybegs to help protect the lorries, as they were some miles apart and the army guard was too small to watch both.

The Station was eventually cleared with the loss of some minor Government stores, by a light lorry under military guard. Throughout two days this vehicle travelled over the mountain road between Glen Bay and Teelin, carrying the stores and Coastguardsmen's furniture which were embarked in H.M. Trawler *Alexander Palmer*.

Before the evacuation the party at Glen Bay were strictly boycotted by the local inhabitants, and could only receive their food supplies from Killybegs – twenty miles away over the mountains. One local man, Mr A. Struthers, helped out by hiring his car for carrying the rations, in spite of continuous threats, but in the end even this method of communication failed because the rebels blocked the roads, and the Glen Bay Station was on very short rations for the last week before evacuation.

Evacuation of BELDERIG COASTGUARD STATION.
H.M. Trawler *Thomas Johns* arrived at 8.15 a.m. and the embarkation was completed at 9.40 p.m.

As the steep descent to the beach precluded the use of vehicles, six men were hired at ten shillings each for the day, and two boys at 2/6d for the half day to assist in carrying furniture. The crew with their personal belongings were taken to Blacksod in the trawler and disembarked at 9 a.m. A caretaker was found to look after the Station building.

'During the evening of the evacuation a crowd assembled from around the countryside and got rather ugly. There were several attempts to loot one cottage and it was necessary to keep them off with a pistol. Had the evacuation lasted until after dark there would almost certainly have been an attack made on the crew,' said the official report.

The Station was fired during that night destroying the lodge and one house. The doors were stolen from the other houses.

On 11th September 1920 the TORR HEAD Coastguard Station and War Signal Station was raided by about fifty disguised, armed men who stole five revolvers, 280 rounds of ammunition, rockets, portfires, four telescopes, two binoculars, the heliograph, and the G.P.O. telephone. The Chief Officer George Timblick later reported that the raid was well planned. The raiders wore rubber on their boots and succeeded in getting five or six men at each door before knocking. They trapped each member of the crew separately.

'I had just retired and I went down at once and asked who was there. I heard someone say "Demand all arms", so I would not open the door but went to the watchroom telephone to report "raided" to the District Officer and to call the watchmen at the War Signal Station, but could get no reply because the wires were cut. I immediately shifted the confidential books, putting them under the table and covering them with signal pads, and succeeded in saving them intact. By then my back door was being burst open. I went down and asked again who was there. Leading Boatman Thomas Hammond replied, "Hammond, Sir, we can do nothing, there are too many of them covering me and will fire if you don't open the door."

'I thought it best to comply and was immediately ordered to put my hands up, and found myself covered by six revolvers.

'Their leader informed me to offer no resistance and they would burn nothing nor interfere with the women and children or private effects. I tried to impress on them that I had nothing of value to them, but they insisted on searching the house, store-room, watchroom and WSS. They made me go to the WSS with them.

'On returning with them I found they had left three men in each house guarding the men. Coastguardsman Morgan was handcuffed but was released on orders of the leader who apologized for keeping them on him so long.

'The leader then ordered everyone to remain in their houses, withdrew his men and informed me that he had taken steps to keep anyone from going to Ballycastle to report the raid.

'The four women and five children were very upset and frightened but were not interfered with in any way, and the leader apologized for causing them inconvenience. He informed me they were soldiers of the Republican Army and their quarrel was with the Government. They seemed well informed as to what they would find at the Station, and several seemed to be men in good position by their talk and dress'.

Torr Head was evacuated on 23rd September and on 6th November the caretaker found the Coastguard building engulfed in flames. It was gutted, but the War Signal Station was not destroyed. The rebels were beaten off when they attacked the Wireless Telegraphy Station at CORKBEG. The station was defended by the crew of four and a detachment of ten Cameron Highlanders. The defenders fired ninety rounds and estimated that the attackers fired two thousand rounds, but there were no casualties reported on either side.

The rebels also had a set-back after burning down the Ballyglass Coastguard Station two days after it had been evacuated. A strong police patrol was on the way to the station at the time and ran into the raiders. Four arrests were made including two notorious leaders of Sinn Fein.

TEELIN 'guarded' Coastguard Station was attacked on 12th June 1921 and a coastguard was killed.

The Sinn Feiners took up position on high ground overlooking the Station and concentrated fire on the windows of the building. The Coastguard returned the fire but because of the weather conditions – it was 3.20 a.m. when the action started – they were unable accurately to sight the enemy. About fifty men were in the attacking party which remained outside the bounds of the station and kept up sniping fire for over an hour. One of the shots killed Coastguard William Kennington. After leaving the Coastguard Station the raiders went to Carrick, about three miles away, and commandeered the only two cars in the place. Local rumour had it that there were five casualties to the raiders.

A week later the 'war' hotted up and on Saturday 18th June

the Coastguard Stations were burned at Malahide, Portrane, Rush, Lough Shinney, Rogertown and Skerries.

Three days later a conference of all Coastguard Divisional Officers in the Kingstown area was held in the office of the Captain of the Division. It was unanimously agreed that until arrangements could be completed for the evacuation of wives and families it was inadvisable to concentrate or make any show of defending certain stations as it was considered that any such movement would be a signal for the destruction of all undefended stations, and that the plight of the wives and families left without any men to help them would be worse than it was already.

The Divisional Officers of Donaghadee and Newcastle stated that the population round their Coastguard Stations were loyal, and that the stations ran practically no danger of being attacked, as this could only come from a flying column which would have to retreat through hostile country and run great danger of being cut off.

It was considered that the wives and families should be evacuated as soon as possible from all stations in Dundalk, Malahide, Kingstown, Wicklow and Wexford Divisions as, following the burning of the Stations in Malahide Division, similar action might be expected at any time in the other South-East divisions.

The conference was told that six families from the burned stations had left for England and the families of twenty-three coastguards had temporary shelter in the homes of neighbouring gentry. Their removal to furnished quarters in England was urgent as most of their worldly possessions had been burnt.

Arrangements were in fact made with the Union Jack Club in Waterloo Road, London to accommodate several destitute families. The attacks on the Coastguard Stations continued until the 'troubles' ended with the setting up of the Irish Free State, and the last Coastguard Station was closed in 1922.

10
Under New Management

The Admiralty, having re-organized the Coastguard immediately after World War 1, kept up the pressure for a decision on the future of the Service.

Already in May 1920 minutes and reports were circulating within the Admiralty, discussing the duties. One memorandum forecast that coast-watching would be necessary in the future and that it should be provided for on any coast where it was possible that an enemy could operate or make use of a harbour for refuge. It was very important that the personnel should be composed of a large percentage of naval men, with many years' experience of coast-watching in peace.

Although the war had been over for a mere eighteen months the navy planners proposed that the coast-watching organization should be worked out locally in detail, so that it could be brought into operation immediately on mobilization, if required.

The naval duties to be performed by the Coastguard were also laid down. These included reporting to certain authorities the movements of all ships of war; suspicious craft whether British, allied, neutral or hostile; to provide a means of communication between the naval authorities and ships and vessels at sea; to patrol the coast, visit remote bays which could not be watched by the Signal Stations, and in general to be a link between the Signal Stations.

The Admiralty then set out the principles on which redistribution of the Coastguard Service should be based.

The sites of Signal Stations should be at focal points of ocean and coastwise traffic. If these were lowlying headlands the site need not be condemned on that account as the introduction of the oxy-acetylene light made a good background less a necessity than formerly. The Signal Stations should also be sited at the entrances to harbours as these stations would then be available as Port War Signal Stations if required. 'In future, with the im-

U.S. Coast Guard Cutter *Vigilant* exercising with gas-turbine powered amphibious helicopter (See chapter fourteen)

R.A.F. Rescue Helicopter hovers while navigator and Coastguard confer (See chapter fourteen)

Modern Coastguard Rescue Headquarters, Deal, Kent (See chapter fourteen)

Coastguards on Look-out (See chapter fourteen)

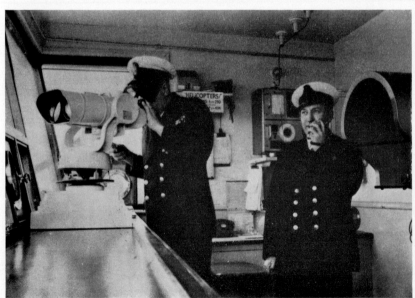

proved signalling which it is hoped will be part of the mercantile marine training, the visual communication with mercantile vessels will be much extended. The resulting economy in pilotage and boat work will ameliorate congestion'.

Signal Stations should also command examination anchorages or the bays, and anchorages where mercantile vessels brought up for different purposes.

Between the War Signal Stations it would be necessary to have certain Stations to carry out War Watching duties, and, where stretches of the coast or likely landing places would be left unwatched or unpatrolled. Sites should be selected or retained and existing stations which would be suitable for the purpose earmarked.

The Admiralty memorandum continued: 'If redistribution on these lines is concurred in, putting it into practice will need much consideration. The Admiralty is not a free agent in the matter because of its obligation, in peace, to assist in life-saving and the protection of the Revenue. Thus in 1908 the Admiralty endeavoured to reduce the Coastguard Force to naval requirements but the opposition from the Treasury was too strong.

'At the best, the process must be gradual, for besides the Customs and life-saving duties, many of the stations which are likely to be considered redundant from the naval point of view carry out multifarious non-naval duties for the Board of Trade, Royal National Lifeboat Institution, Ministry of Agriculture and Fisheries, etc.

'The scheme for the Coastguard Stations being taken over by the Board of Trade and manned by a pensioner force has never been put to the Treasury, but it would seem open to exactly the same objections from the Treasury point of view as the former scheme for the Customs to take over the stations.

'As far as the Admiralty are concerned it would not appear to matter whether Customs take them and do Board of Trade work, or the Board of Trade take them and do Customs work.

'It is to be observed that the Coastguard is now reorganized as a pensioner force. This would seem to weaken some of the previous Admiralty arguments as against the Board of Trade, the men no longer being withdrawn on mobilization. The question would therefore now seem to be chiefly financial – how much

Navy Votes should be called upon to bear at the demand of the Board of Trade.

'On the other hand the main reason for the Coastguard being turned over from Customs to Admiralty in 1856 seems to have disappeared i.e., the training of a Reserve Naval Force'.

Having formulated their policy, the Admiralty wrote to the Treasury on 9th April 1921 on the functions and cost of the Coastguard Service with reference to the requirements of H.M. Navy, and 'the present urgent need for economy'.

The pre-war Coastguard was considered an important reserve for H.M. Navy. It was arranged that in time of war the entire force, with the exception of those employed in Wireless Telegraphy Stations and a certain number of Coastguard Stations called War Signal Stations which were of especial importance in time of war, should be drafted to serve afloat.

In actual practice this proved not to be a satisfactory arrangement. Immediately after the outbreak of war it was necessary to organize *de novo* a coast-watching force all round the coast of the United Kingdom. It would have been more satisfactory if the Coastguard Force, so far as it was not required for W.S. Stations and W.T. Stations, had been allowed to remain on outbreak of war to form the nucleus of this coast-watching force.

At the same time the experience of war showed that the Coastguard did not form an essential part of the Naval Reserve and that it would be quite sufficient to rely on personnel supplied in the ordinary course by the R.N.R., Royal Fleet Reserve and the R.N.V.R.

The Second Sea Lord in a Minute dated 30th December 1921 recorded that of the 419 Coastguard Stations, 144 were not required by the Admiralty for its own purposes, and they had arranged to close sixteen by agreement with the Board of Trade and the Board of Customs and Excise. This would leave 128 which the Navy did not require.

'Even so there will still be 275 Coastguard Stations doing heterogeneous duty for other Government Departments, Trinity House and Lloyds with a small amount of naval work in the form of reports to the Hydrographer and recruiting for the Navy.

'The Naval Staff have laid down that the peace complement of 3,000 trained coastguards is the minimum required for manning War Signal Stations and forming the nucleus of a coast-watching organization in war, reinforced by the Coastguard Reserve.

'The training of Coastguard in their war duties is as necessary in peace as training naval personnel generally, and there is the added advantage that the Coastguard perform beneficial duties in peace, in addition to their naval duties, thus curtailing the expenses of other departments whose staff otherwise would have to be largely augmented.

'One of the principal non-naval duties is in connection with life-saving apparatus round the coast for the Board of Trade. The life-saving apparatus is in almost all cases in charge of the Coastguard who keep the necessary look-out in bad weather, and are responsible for calling out the Life-saving Apparatus Company and, informing the Lifeboat Authorities of any casualty at sea.'

The Admiralty had apparently accepted the necessity for the Coastguard to perform these non-naval duties when, in 1922, the 'Geddes Axe' was poised over the Service.

The Committee on National Expenditure in their first interim report singled out the Coastguard for comment.

'The 128 Coastguard Stations left which the Navy say they do not require for their own purposes, we recommend should be reconsidered by the Board of Customs, the Board of Trade and the Post Office, who are primarily concerned in these stations, and they should suggest a further reduction. The other 275 Coastguard Stations do not have sufficient justification from the naval point of view and we think that the *onus probandi* must be laid upon the other Departments of the Government, and that they should meanwhile be strongly pressed to reduce these stations to the barest minimum, unless serious loss of revenue due to smuggling is to be apprehended, and, if they require them the cost should be noted on their Estimates'.

The Geddes Committee recommended that the Coastguard should be cut to 1,500 men and a Naval Staff Conference was convened on 6th January 1922 to discuss the recommendation. In framing their Report the Conference was asked to consider the urgent need of economy and Cabinet advice that there was no likelihood of Great Britain being involved in a war of any magnitude, particularly with a European power before 1929.

The Conference laid down the requirements in Coastguard personnel for purely naval duties as:

England and Scotland	Ireland	Total	Reduction in Personnel
345	nil	345	2,655

Stations to be manned in peacetime:

Wireless Telegraphy	12	a reduction of 8
Direction Finding	1	a reduction of 5
Port War Signal	7	a reduction of 30
War Signal	nil	a reduction of 83
Coastguard	nil	a reduction of 337

The members of the Conference reiterated that the reductions were with the proviso that the matter had been examined from a purely naval point of view, and no consideration had been taken of other Government Departments such as Customs and Board of Trade etc. This forced the issue and the whole matter was turned over for investigation by an Interdepartmental Committee, in 1922, to 'inquire and report what establishment is necessary for carrying out the civil duties of revenue protection, life-saving coast-watching, etc. now discharged by the Coastguard'.

The Committee recommended the suspension, in times of peace, of the Coastguard as such and the substitution of:

1. A Naval Signalling Section for the purpose of manning such stations as are considered necessary to conform with naval requirements. The cost to be borne on Naval Votes.

2. A Coast-watching force to perform duties in connection with the saving of life, the salvage of wreck, and the administration of foreshores and certain miscellaneous duties. The cost to be borne on the Vote of the Board of Trade.

3. Coast Preventive force to supplement the existing Waterguard staff to perform duties in connection with the protection of the revenue. The cost being borne on the Customs and Excise Vote.

It further recommended that on the outbreak of war the Naval

Signalling Section of the Coast-Watching force should be placed under the orders of the Admiralty as a Coastguard Service.

The Force to be maintained by the Board of Trade should consist of a total personnel of 935 and, with the exception of twelve Divisional Inspectors, that they should all be housed at the expense of the State at 322 existing Coastguard Stations.

The staff of 935 should include the men required for coast-watching at stations where, under a contract extending to 1951, the Admiralty carried out commercial signalling for Lloyds.

The Committee also recommended that the housing and other accommodation required for the coast-watching service should be placed under control of H.M. Office of Works and the cost borne on the Vote for Public Works and Buildings.

The Report was adopted by the Government and there was an immediate public outcry led by the *Fortnightly Review,* which in November, 1922, under the heading 'The abolition of the Coastguard' declared: It is proposed to abolish the Coastguard which Admiral Lord Beresford once described as the backbone of the Navy, and in place of this one force which at present carries out many and varied duties to establish three bodies to do the same work.

Since the Coastguard exists for the defence of the coast and the saving of life from shipwreck, as well as the prevention of smuggling, it is not a little remarkable that the Committee should have included no member practically conversant with the essential duties which it performs on behalf of a community which must be defended from the sea if it is to be defended at all, and which, if it is to live must live by the sea, making every possible provision, as a matter of duty, for the safeguarding of shipping and the rescue of passengers and crews from drowning.

Neither the Navy, the mercantile marine, the R.N.L.I., Lloyd's which largely depends upon the Coastguard for reports of casualties, nor Trinity House, was represented on the Committee.

Though the Report extends to nearly one hundred pages, the public is left in ignorance of the character of the evidence which was taken, and there is nothing to suggest that any naval officers concerned with the organization and administration of the Coastguard in the past, any of the bodies which watch over the interest of merchant officers and men, any representatives of the general

133

body of shipowners, any member of the Committee of Lloyds, or any of the Elder Brethren of Trinity House were consulted before it was decided practically to sweep away an organization which has deserved well of this maritime nation, and has formed a valuable link between it and the force 'upon which, under the good providence of God, the wealth, prosperity and peace of these islands and of the Empire do mainly depend'.

The constitution of the Coastguard force has varied, but today it performs more important and varied duties than at any previous time in its history. The public has little conception of the many responsibilities which in course of time have been thrown upon it.

They include duties in peacetime for the Admiralty:

1. Communication between the Fleet and the Admiralty by Wireless Telegraphy and visual signalling.

2. Intelligence: information is telegraphed to the Admiralty of the arrivals, sailings and movements of foreign ships of war. Movements of H.M. Ships are reported to the local C-in-C. Reports are made to the Admiral Commanding Coastguard and Reserves of important occurrences on or near the coast.

3. Recruiting: men and boys are recruited for the Navy. Candidates are examined for the R.N.R. Pensioners are examined as to fitness for mobilization. Addresses of R.N. reservists are verified.

Hydrography: reports are made to the Hydographer of all changes in positions or visibility of buoys and beacons. The erection of piers or buildings likely to be useful to navigation. The occurrence of abnormally high or low tides and the weather conditions prevailing at the time. The site of any good landing place not mentioned in Sailing Directions.

Mines: At certain stations a mine expert is stationed for the purpose of rendering mines safe.

Miscellaneous: The investigation of claims rendered in respect of damage caused to fishing nets by H.M. Ships.

It is responsible to the Customs and Excise for the boarding of vessels and search for dutiable goods at places where there are no Customs Officers; the searching of fishing vessels and boats; the patrol of the coasts, creeks, etc.; the issue of certificates of health to vessels or the detention of vessels which may be suspected or infected where there are no Customs Officers, and the provision of boats for the Medical Officers of Health.

Over and above these duties the Coastguard, on behalf of the Board of Trade, renders assistance to ships in distress and carries out measures for the preservation of life and property, taking charge of wrecked goods which are dutiable; receives distress messages from lighthouses and lightships, testing daily the electrical communications and notifying interruptions; reports all wrecks and casualties and takes charge of nearly all the rocket life-saving apparatus and of the Companies working it, part of the crews being provided from the ratings available; gives constant attendance at the coast communication telephones and exercises a general supervision over the foreshores in the interests of the Crown, as well as of all those who go down to the sea in ships.

Post Office: The transaction of public telegraph business in remote places. Assistance is given to certain P.O. Wireless Stations.

Fishery Departments: The collection of statistical returns relating to the quantity and value of fish landed. The enforcement of the provisions of the Sea Fisheries Acts. Reports are made on the encroachment of foreign fishing vessels. The detection of trawling within the three-mile limit.

In Ireland only, reports are made to the conservators of any infringement of the Salmon Fishing bye-laws.

Information is supplied respecting mackerel and herring fishings.

Air Ministry: The care of meteorological instruments at certain stations and the report of observations made with them. Returns of air and sea temperatures are rendered from certain stations. The operation of storm warning signals.

Agricultural Departments: The enforcement of the regulations concerning the landing of dogs and other animals.

Royal National Lifeboat Institution: Station Officers serve as

135

members of the Local Committees and ratings may form part of the lifeboat crews. Immediate information is given to the nearest lifeboats of all vessels observed in distress. Information is given to neighbouring lifeboats if a lifeboat is prevented for any reason from rendering assistance.

Trinity House: Commissioners of Northern Lighthouses (Scotland); Commissioners of Irish Lighthouses: reports are made in case of shifting buoys, fallen beacons, drifting light-vessels and the failure or irregularity of lights.

Home Office, Scottish Office and the Society for the protection of Wild Birds: Warnings are given to persons seen breaking the law, and reports are made to the police if necessary.

Lloyds: Commercial maritime signalling at certain stations for which payment is made by Lloyds. Telegraphic reports of all casualties.

In the knowledge of all this work which is carried out by the Coastguard, the Inter-departmental Committee recommends a scheme of reorganization which is equivalent practically to the abolition of the force. This conclusion is all the more remarkable in view of the admissions which are made in the report, all pointing to the importance of retaining a well-drilled and highly efficient force, under discipline, in the interests of the country at large, since, in spite of the development of air power, this is still an island liable to invasion, and in the interest also of the officers and men of the Royal Navy and the mercantile marine, and all who have occasion to travel by sea for business or pleasure.

Lifesaving Apparatus Stations have been provided all round the coast at 294 points, look-out huts erected at suitable points, and an almost complete network of coastal telephones established between the Apparatus Stations, the Coastguard Stations, the look-out huts and the lifeboats of the R.N.L.I. which number 256. 'In bad weather a continuous day and night watch is essential from a sufficient number of points to ensure that the coastline and adjacent waters are kept under close observation'. Except at a few places, this watch is at present maintained by the Coastguard whose duty it is, if any ship is observed to be in difficulty, to report at once to the nearest Apparatus Station and the lifeboat coxswain. The Coastguard also keep the Apparatus in order and take part in working it, while the Coastguard officers are responsible for the training of the Apparatus Companies in their duties.

The R.N.L.I. depends very largely on the Coastguard watch and on the coast communication telephone for information regarding wrecks or vessels in distress for which their lifeboats are needed.

We understand that as recently as March last, the Institution urged, in a deputation to the President of the Board of Trade, that the present facilities should not only be maintained but should be substantially improved.

The Committee also considered there was a need for a disciplined force provided with and accustomed to use arms. The Merchant Shipping Act 1894 empowers the Receiver of Wreck, in the event of wreck being plundered to use force if necessary. The Act assumed the existence of an adequate and disciplined body to carry out its provisions, and the Board of Trade might be held responsible by the owners and underwriters of wrecked vessels or property for any failure to provide sufficient force to prevent plunder. The Coastguard acts as Receivers of Wreck.

After setting out the Committee's proposals the article points out that under the proposed scheme seventy-four coastguard stations would be closed and let to weekenders.

'What, it may be asked lies behind the report of this Interdepartmental Committee? The answer is a simple one – interdepartmental differences. The Navy Votes bear the whole cost of maintaining this force, and that is obviously an improper arrangement, but that admission need not surely involve the breaking up of the Coastguard Service with its fine traditions'.

Two Admirals were moved to comment on the proposed changes.

Admiral Sir Cecil Thursby, at one time Admiral Commanding Coastguard and Reserves, thought it might be possible to abolish the Coastguard without risk, but not until arrangements had been made to man the chain of coastal wireless stations, to provide a system of visual signalling from the shore stations to patrol vessels and submarine chasers not fitted with wireless, and to establish systems of coastwatching and coast communications. 'When all these essential services have been provided for I doubt very much whether it will be possible to make any considerable saving in practice, whatever may be the effect of calculations on paper'.

Paymaster Rear-Admiral W. E. R. Martin, who had served in the Coastguard, had misgivings about the wisdom of splitting up the Coastguard force into different bodies under multiple control. 'From war experience I can imagine the confusion that will ensue when the Board of Trade and the Customs hand over to the Admiralty the control of their men on the outbreak of war.

'All my experience teaches me that peace organizations must be capable of instant development for war purposes, and the recommendations of the Committee would not admit of this, if the Government were to enforce them as they now appear.

'The Committee's scheme cannot be carried out without asking Parliament to repeal the Coastguard Service Act of 1856, and if this course be attempted there is reason to hope that the House of Commons, reflecting public opinion, will refuse to sanction proposals which in fact promise only a small economy, and that economy at the expense of the efficient watching of our coasts.

'This Inter-departmental Committee has however rendered one good service. It has reminded the nation of the varied and important duties which are performed by the Coastguard under peace conditions, while, at the same time, admitting that when war comes, even the present strength will prove inadequate for the efficient protection of this country.

'The solution of the problem is surely to be found in a simple scheme of financial readjustment between the various departments and for the rest, the responsibility should remain with the Admiralty of ensuring that the Coastguard is maintained in the highest state of efficiency'.

In the face of such opposition the Government did adopt the report and when on 1st April 1923 the Board of Trade assumed responsibility for coast-watching, they based their organization mainly upon the recommendations contained in the report. However, to mollify public opinion, by Royal Sanction the Force retained the title of His Majesty's Coastguard.

The change took place by administrative action, and in 1925 a new Coastguard Act was passed to regularize the transfer. This Act repealed the Act of 1856, and Section 1 (1) of the new Act provided that 'H.M. Coastguard shall consist of such numbers of officers and men as the Board of Trade may, with the consent of the Treasury, from time to time think fit, and shall be raised, maintained, equipped and governed by the Board and employed as a Coast-watching Force for the performance of the duties hitherto performed on behalf of the Board and of such other duties as may be determined by the Board'.

Section 2 provided that 'Whenever any emergency arises which, in the opinion of the Admiralty renders it advisable that H.M. Coastguard shall be placed under the control of the Admiralty, the Admiralty may by order direct that the management and control of H.M. Coastguard shall be transferred to the Admiralty'.

11
The Loss of the Islander

The Coastguard Act which transferred the Coastguard to the
control of the Board of Trade brought a radical change of
emphasis to the service. For the first time the country had a
specialist organization devoted to life-saving and coast-watching.
The new force was taken over for administrative purposes by
the Mercantile Marine Division of the Board which had the
telegraphic address 'Shipminder, London', an apt description of
the function of the Coastguard.

The 1922 Committee contemplated the coast-watching service
as being confined to stations which had been manned by the
Admiralty Coastguard. They expressed the view that 'in bad
weather a continuous watch, day and night, was essential from
a sufficient number of points to ensure that the coastline and
adjacent waters were kept under observation', but, although the
list of stations which they recommended for retention left long
stretches of the coast unwatched, no suggestions were made by
them for the provision of any additional coast-watching stations.

The Board of Trade interpreted their main task as being
that of providing an adequate coast-watching organization in bad
or thick weather, taking into account the modern changes in
shipping conditions including the great reduction in the number
of sailing vessels, improved facilities for communication both on
shore and at sea, and, the development of modern aids to navigation including the use of wireless for directional and other
purposes.

As a result of a careful examination of requirements and existing conditions it was found that the proposals made in the 1922
Report were not entirely satisfactory. The Board decided that
the best policy was to provide:

(*a*) Well manned stations at the main danger points of the
coasts.

(*b*) Stations with smaller staffs at less dangerous places.

(*c*) Auxiliary Stations generally based on somewhat widely spaced Coastguard Stations occupying commanding positions in relation to shipping traffic on less important parts of the coast.

The stations in (*a*) and (*b*) being manned by regularly employed men, and, those in (*c*) by local people under the charge of a responsible resident who in turn would normally receive his instructions for setting watch from a regular Coastguard Station.

The new Coastguard Service was designed primarily for keeping watch in bad weather and the Board of Trade in consultation with the R.N.L.I. adopted the principle that watch should be set when the conditions were such that, if a casualty should occur on the coast there was an element of risk to the lives of the crew of the vessel if, either, they remained on board, or they attempted to land in their own boats or by other means available from resources on board.

In applying this principle and for the guidance of the staff employed in the organization they defined bad weather as:

(*a*) General: 'On shore' wind force exceeding that of a moderate breeze.

(*b*) Particular: 1. When conditions of wind and sea or tide render landing by boats on the open beach hazardous, although the force of wind may be less than a moderate breeze and may not be 'on shore'.

2. When, in the vicinity of harbours, especially those concerned with fishing, conditions of wind, weather or tide render approach dangerous.

The wind definition was adopted by the Board to ensure that as far as possible watch should be set before the conditions set forth in the principle were operative.

It was also provided that watch should be set, mainly for warning purposes, in thick weather or in conditions of low visability, 'Thick Weather' being defined as:

(*a*) General: When visability is one mile or less.

(*b*) Particular: When outlying rocks or shoals, visible under normal conditions are not visible from look-out posts.

When lighthouses or light-vessels either within sight under normal conditions or connected to stations electrically are sounding their fog signals.

The general standard adopted by the Board of Trade was that lookout should be maintained from a sufficient number of points to ensure, with reasonable certainty, that any efficient visual or sound signals from vessels in distress, danger or difficulty would be observed in order that assistance of a suitable character might be dispatched without delay, or that any vessel which might be observed standing into danger could be warned by signal, foghorn etc. of her position.

To ensure the maintenance of this standard it was necessary to arrange for at least one station in any area to be placed on watch at night, irrespective of the weather conditions so that watch could be set at the other stations on the approach of bad or thick weather.

Apart from ensuring 'bad weather watch' and general supervision at night it was considered that in certain localities more was needed. These included the Goodwins, the approaches to the Thames Estuary and the shoals off the Norfolk and Suffolk coasts where vessels may, and in fact do run into dangers in all weathers. In such localities provision was made for the maintenance of constant watch both day and night. The communications were improved in co-operation with the Lighthouse Authorities by providing radio telephony on lightships and at lighthouses as well as at selected Coastguard Stations.

The general organization of the service adopted by the Board of Trade was designed to provide an adequate and competent staff on the coast, administered and controlled from headquarters in London. The maintenance of watch at an adequate number of Coastguard Look-outs sited in commanding positions. The establishment of Auxiliary watching stations on stretches of coast where Coastguard Stations could not be justified. The proper control of the stations and of watchkeeping. Adequate telephone facilities and other means of communication necessary for a comprehensive intelligence system, including liaison with other organizations. The co-ordination of life-saving activities and co-operation with the R.N.L.I. The installation of effective life-saving appliances, and, the training and inspection by officers of the Coastguard of Companies to work the life-saving apparatus.

The performance of various miscellaneous duties for the Board of Trade and other Government Departments. The recruitment and training of personnel best qualified to perform the duties required of the organization and their employment under reasonable conditions of service.

All matters relating to policy and general administration of the service, and with the recruitment of new personnel were to be dealt with by the Board in London. The Chief Inspector and Deputy Chief Inspector would be stationed in London and act as advisers to the Board. They were to make periodical visits to the coast, and in normal circumstances one or the other would visit every station once a year.

One of the first acts intended to improve morale in the new Coastguard was the introduction, in 1923, of the 'Wreck Service Shield' to be presented annually to the Life-saving Company performing the most meritorious wreck service during the year. To further encourage members of the Life-saving Companies, men who had served for at least twenty years and had been regular and prompt in attendance at wreck services and exercises qualified for the Long Service Medal, approved for the Coastguard by King George V in 1911.

The first holders of the Shield, which soon became regarded as the blue riband of life-saving, was the Blyth Life-saving Company.

On the night of 16th February 1923 during a south-easterly gale, a Coastguard at Blyth saw distress signals from the steamer *Laurence* of 297 tons, which was aground near the entrance to the harbour.

The Lifeboat Authority was informed and a maroon was fired to call out the Life-saving Company. As the men were assembling a passing taxi was hailed, and the Coastguard and as many members of the company as could pack inside were driven a mile to the ferry, and crossed the river to the rocket-cart house. The cart was hauled by hand a mile to the end of the pier and on a space of ten feet the apparatus was set up. Within half an hour of the start of the operation a rocket was fired.

The vessel was end-on to the pier and it required the firing of three rockets before a line went over the ship. Because of the high seas the crew were unable to signal that they had made the line fast, but the breeches buoy was sent out over the rocks on which the seas were breaking. The entire crew of fourteen was rescued in an hour. The ship went to pieces during the night.

The trophy, with the name Blyth engraved in the first space, was later handed over to the president of the Company by the Chief Inspector of Coastguard, Captain J. D. Daintree, at a ceremony in the Town Hall.

The award of the shield to the North Berwick company in 1927 highlighted the appalling conditions which face the Coastguard and life-savers on the east coast of Scotland.

On Boxing Day 1927 a Belgian steamer the S.S. *Charles* was sailing down the Firth of Forth, in ballast, in a force 5–8 northeast gale, with a heavy swell and blinding snow squalls.

At 8.45 a.m. the vessel was seen between the islands of Fidra and Lamb, with anchor down and steaming full ahead. The Coastguard, seeing the plight of the vessel, called out the L.S.A. Company, and, shortly afterwards the ship parted her cable and stranded three-quarters of a mile west of Fidra.

At 9.20 a.m. the company left their station, hauling the wagon by hand. The horses which had been summoned were met after a mile, but as a lorry passed at the same time and there was still three miles to go, the lorry was used to tow the apparatus and the horses followed on behind.

The last mile to the scene of the wreck was over and through snow-drifts with the men dragging, lifting and pushing the cart until finally it was bogged down a quarter of a mile from the point opposite the wreck. The gear had then to be carried for the last part of the journey.

The *Charles* was stranded six hundred yards below high-water mark so the gear was taken over the rocks to within two hundred yards, and a rocket was fired. As the tide was rising rapidly it became urgent to get the crew ashore. The whip gear and the triangle were lashed to the rocks and the crew of fourteen were landed, but not without problems. As the tide rose the gear had to be moved from rock to rock, and members of the company worked waist deep in the water.

When the eleventh man was landed the breeches buoy parted, and there was no time to do more than lash the parts together. The last three members of the crew were then brought ashore holding the slings and sitting on the broken buoy. Throughout the operation the gale continued to blow with heavy hail and snow at times.

In 1929 the Shield was shared by two Companies, each holding it for six months.

The Hope Cove, Devon, L.S.A. had a grim tale to tell of conditions on 12th February 1928 when they rescued the crew of the S.S. *Deventia* of Workington (364 tons).

At 12.50 a.m. the Hope Cove Coastguard on duty at Greystone Look-out saw distress signals from a vessel to the east and called the District Officer, Hope Cove. He called out the L.S.A. Company and an advance party, in a lorry, took the communication gear and located the ship one and a half miles west of Bolt Head. It was intensely cold and the ground was covered with a thin layer of ice. An easterly gale force six–seven was blowing accompanied by driving snow.

The wagon could not be taken the full distance to the wreck because of the weather, and the gear had to be carried a mile along the cliff-tops. So dangerous was the icy ground, with the wind tugging at their clothes and the ever present fear of slipping over the high cliffs that the men rigged life-lines and crawled on their hands and knees over some parts of the journey.

The first rocket was fired at 3.35 a.m. but the ship could scarcely be seen owing to the intense darkness and driving snow. The acetylene lamps had frozen and the company had to rig the apparatus in the dark, but they managed to get a line to the ship with the second rocket at 4 a.m. Cotton waste soaked in paraffin was set on fire to give enough light to work the gear.

There was no way in which those on shore could see when a member of the crew entered the breeches buoy and was ready to be hauled in, and a large rock made it impossible to haul the breeches buoy with a passenger with safety to the top of the cliff on which they were working. The only solution was for the breeches buoy to be hauled out to the ship and held long enough for one of the crew to climb in, and then hauled to a point 150 feet from the top of the cliff and again held until the passenger landed.

When day broke the company found that they had rescued three members of the crew who were then helped to the top of the cliff with life-lines. The Plymouth lifeboat arrived and took off the remaining ten members of the crew.

The Newhaven L.S.A. Company shared the Shield for their rescue from the S.S. *Merwede* of Rotterdam (180 tons) which went aground one and a half miles east of Newhaven in a force 9–10 westerly gale on 6 December 1928 in exceptionally heavy seas. The vessel was seen by the Newhaven Coastguard trying to make for the harbour and the lifeboat was launched but was forced to return to harbour.

At 8.15 p.m. the lights on board became obscured and it was realized that the *Merwede* had missed the harbour and was in imminent danger.

A coastguardsman was sent off on a motor-cycle to locate the wreck and the Newhaven L.S.A. Company was called out and went to the shore in a lorry. The advance party saw a coastguard light burning half a mile to the east of the road leading to the beach and the life-saving gear was then manhandled along the beach.

The first rocket was blown off course by the gale but, after the apparatus was moved to a new position, the second rocket carried a line over the ship. The heavy seas breaking over the vessel prevented the crew from reaching the line and a third rocket was fired. This dropped the line over the aft part where the crew were sheltering, and the breeches buoy was hauled off.

The vessel was ashore by the stern and rolling heavily as each sea struck her so it required careful judgement in working the whip to prevent the man in the breeches buoy from being dashed on the beach. The entire crew of eleven were landed in fifty minutes by the life-saving company working up to their waists in the sea.

By 1930 the Coastguard and the Life-saving Apparatus Companies had been welded by the Board of Trade into a highly efficient coast-watching and rescue team, and the men were proud of the high esteem in which they were held by the public, when an event occurred which was to call that efficiency into question.

The *Islander* was a wooden carvel-built vessel of about twenty-two tons, forty-three feet long, built in 1911 and at one time a Bristol pilot cutter. Ralph Stock went round the world in her and afterwards wrote *The Cruise of the Dreamship*.

In 1921 she was fitted with a two-cylinder motor which gave her a speed of about four knots in fine weather, and, although she was converted into a yacht she remained cutter rigged.

The *Islander* was bought in 1928 by Lieutenant-Colonel John Neston Diggle who, on 8th, August 1930, chartered her to Commodore H. Douglas King, D.S.O., Conservative member of Parliament for South Paddington and a former Secretary for Mines and A.D.C. to the King.

At about 7 a.m. on 20th August the *Islander* sailed from Dartmouth for Falmouth with Commodore King, Captain R. C. Glazebrook a farmer from Essex, Surgeon-Captain A. R. Brailey, honorary surgeon to the King, and Commander Sidney Searle, who was Lieutenant Commander in H.M.S. *Iron Duke* at the battle of Jutland, as passengers, and the two-man crew H. W. Lucas the master and W. R. S. Lucas. The weather was fine and nothing further was known of the yacht's movements until about 7 p.m. that evening when a fisherman at Polperro saw her steering in a north-westerly direction, fairly close in, and a second fisherman some distance along the coast also reported seeing her. It was blowing strongly, the sea was rough and there was intermittent rain.

A farmer looking out to sea observed the yacht which was keeping close to land. He last saw her near Bell Buoy which marked a dangerous rock known as the Udder Rock, about a mile from the shore. The rock had about three feet of water over it at low tide and the *Islander* drew about eight feet five inches.

The farmer thought that the vessel would pass between the rock and the shore if she did not sail over it, and when he lost sight of her she was proceeding at a good speed.

On the cliffs in Lantivit Bay, about 700 yards west of Island Rock, there was a camping party led by a Dr Fox. At about 8.30 p.m. a member of the party drew Dr Fox's attention to a light on the Bell Buoy. The doctor thought it was a flare that might be from a vessel in distress near the buoy and ran to the home of Mr Ralph Roseveare a farmer. They got into a car parked in a field near the house, intending to drive to Polruan to raise the alarm but, unfortunately, the car was almost immediately bogged down.

The two men then ran to the next house where Mr Roseveare's

father lived, and he got his car out and drove to Polruan where he gave the alarm to the Coastguard on watch.

The Coastguard immediately telephoned the Secretary of the lifeboat and the Coastguard Station Officer, and fired two maroons followed by a third as signals to launch the lifeboat and call out the Life-saving Apparatus Company. Members of the company appeared within minutes and some of the equipment was loaded into a car. Members of the company set off in other cars with the rest of the equipment.

The lifeboat was manned within ten minutes and sailed for Lantivet Bay where, while it was searching for the *Islander* the L.S.A. company arrived in the cars, after experiencing great difficulty crossing the fields to the cliff-top. The equipment was set up and a rocket was fired but missed the tiny target.

The lifeboat picked up the *Islander* in her searchlight. She was only two hundred yards from the rocks, in breaking water, and the lifeboat went in as close as possible, anchored and tried to fire a line to the yacht but it fell short. The official enquiry held later reported, 'It was quite impossible for the lifeboat to proceed further in, and her failure to be able to render assistance was due to one thing only, that through no fault of her own she arrived too late'.

While the alarm was being raised by Mr Roseveare senior, Mr Ralph Roseveare went back to the cliff edge and saw flares, made from clothing soaked in paraffin, being burned on the *Islander*. Two figures could be seen on deck and the yacht had an anchor down but was dragging.

Mr Roseveare, with a Mr Eddy, climbed down the cliff to a cove where some small ropes were kept in boats. They then went with several members of the L.S.A. company along the cliff to Island Rock. The yacht had dragged right in to the rock and was rising and falling in the heavy sea bumping her stern against the rocks.

The master was forward and his brother was lying on the deck. Apparently crowding on the seats in the cockpit were four people covered up for shelter. The yacht's deck was clear, no sails, boom or gaff were seen.

One of the rescuers, Mr Hunt, stood on Island Rock and threw a rope across the yacht and this was caught by Lucas and his brother who made it fast. Before any rescue could be effected a heavy sea struck the craft and the Rock, driving Mr Hunt and Mr Roseveare back. Mr Hunt then called to the yacht for a larger rope and the master fetched one from a locker and bent the small rope to it.

The men on the rock hauled it ashore but before it could be secured another heavy sea struck the *Islander* and the backwash carried her out. She swung to starboard heading for the shore, grounded on a rocky ledge. Another wave struck her and slipping off, she foundered. Throughout the entire rescue attempt the four figures in the cockpit remained motionless and it was thought that they had been injured when the *Islander* struck Udder Rock and was dismasted.

Where was the Coastguard during the emergency? This was investigated at length by the Inquiry and brought serious criticism of the system of coast-watching in force.

Overlooking Lantivet Bay, with a full view of the Bell Buoy was a Coastguard hut which, if manned, was manned by Coastguards from Polruan Coastguard Station. The hut was connected by telephone to the station and, had it been manned as it should have been, the alarm would have reached Polruan Coastguard Station shortly after 8.30 p.m., and nearly an hour would have been saved.

'It is impossible to say that if the alarm had been given when it should have been the yacht and the lives of those on board her would necessarily have been saved. All that can be said is that the chances of success would have been very greatly increased' declared the Court of Inquiry.

The reason that there was no bad weather watch at the Lantivit look-out hut was attributed to the orders of the District Officer, who had modified the system in his District in April 1930. This introduced what the Court described as the 'alternative' system which had as its object that in clear but bad weather, so far as sea and wind were concerned, watchkeeping was dispensed with at some of the Stations whose coastline and waters, in clear visibility, could be seen from adjacent Stations which were kept on watch.

The Court understood that the system had proved to be a good system if properly worked, where, in daylight and in clear weather, two Stations could overlook the coast and waters of an intermediate Station. It was not a suitable system when visibility was bad, nor, except in very exceptional circumstances, was it a system suitable at night.

For its successful operation three conditions were essential.

1. The look-out Stations to be combined must be carefully selected so as to ensure that the Stations keeping watch in bad weather could overlook the coasts and waters of the Station not keeping bad weather watch.
2. The District Officer controlling the system must have full knowledge of the weather existing at the various Stations and the changes that might take place.
3. The very closest co-operation was required between the District Officer and the various Stations so that the dispositions he had made as to bad weather watch could be quickly altered should circumstances require it.

'In this particular instance not one of these conditions was complied with', the Court decided.

The Court pointed out that serious as were the errors committed by the District Officer, they had their origin in mistaken and misplaced zeal, and not in conscious or wilful neglect of duty. The Divisional Inspector and the Station Officer at Fowey were also criticized, and the Court of Inquiry ended its report with a suggestion that in view of the errors and omissions which had been disclosed, a more comprehensive inquiry was desirable.

At the inquest on Commodore King and Commander Searle, Sir Arthur Quiller-Couch gave evidence about conditions on the coast. He thought that the system of coast-watching and patrolling was insufficient, and consequently must be comparatively inefficient.

In reply to the coroner, he said that if anyone had been on duty in the watch-house at Lantivet Bay they would have seen the signals of distress. 'In the old days of the Coastguards, when there was a different service altogether, this thing would never have happened. I think it is attributable to Government action in reducing Coastguards and staffs. A watch on the sea is more necessary in summer than in winter, because vessels which come along in the winter are commanded by master mariners, but the craft which swarm off the coast in the summer are often handled by holidaymakers who do not understand their handling.

After returning a verdict of accidental death by drowning, the jury added a rider – 'the jury considers that on this particular evening there was a laxity in the placing of the watches. Without doubt there should have been a watch set earlier in the evening at Lantivet, and also a constant watch should be kept on the hill at Polruan'.

The adverse comments led to public criticism of the adequacy and efficiency of the entire coast-watching organization, and although the Board of Trade considered the comments to be un-justified, an independent Departmental Committee of Inquiry was set up under the chairmanship of Admiral Sir George Hope, K.G.B., K.C.M.G. The Committee carried out a very thorough investigation before presenting their report to Parliament in July 1931.

The Committee recorded that they were impressed by the relative absence of any adverse criticisms from those parties most likely to be affected by any failure to maintain an efficient Coastguard Service.

One witness on the question of personnel stated that 'In the Coastguard Service you have one of the finest services you can get, the finest the country can produce. They are men who have been tried and unless they are really fit they do not get positions'.

From their examination of the conditions on certain parts of the coast the Committee formed the opinion that the retention of Coastguard Stations on unfrequented parts of the coast merely to maintain continuity of the watching organization could not be justified and that such stations should either be closed or reduced to auxiliary stations for use in bad or thick weather only.

'We also consider that the maintenance, at the cost of the State, of Coastguard Stations on parts of the coast frequented mainly by holiday traffic in summer is not justified and we recommend that existing stations falling under this head should be closed, reduced to auxiliary stations or maintained at the expense of the local authority or authorities of the pleasure resorts concerned. If local authorities or bodies desire a watch-ing organization for the protection of pleasure craft at seaside resorts we think it is not unreasonable that they should themselves bear the cost of providing and maintaining the necessary look-outs'.

In general the Committee agreed with the Board of Trade that constant watch was desirable in certain circumstances and that even in fine weather a proportion of the staff should be on duty at night to provide general supervision over traffic routes. They found that the system of providing night watches in fine weather had been arranged by grouping three stations and placing them on duty in turn. 'As stations differ in their relative importance according to their position on the coast this system is not the most satisfactory method of affording the necessary general supervision at night, because on some nights it involves the maintenance of watch from stations which supervise comparatively unimportant sections of coasts while stations in much better positions are not on duty. We think a better method would be to select those stations which by reason of their situation afford the greatest amount of supervision of the coast and sea and place them on regular night duty, leaving the remaining and necessarily less important stations to be set on watch when weather deteriorates or visibility falls.

'We recommend therefore that stations should be classified according to the importance of their situation in relation to the normal movements of shipping, this classification being subject to review from time to time so as to keep in line with changes in conditions.

(*a*) Constant Watch Stations: These would necessarily be limited in number as it is only where there are serious dangers to navigation or where stations are near the more important ports, with a constant flow of traffic, that day and night watch is required irrespective of weather conditions.

(*b*) Constant Night Watch Stations. In commanding positions: In fine weather night watch would be kept for a group of stations to ensure that the maximum supervision called for in the circumstances is afforded. These stations would also, in bad weather or periods of low visibility, set watch by day.

(*c*) Other Coastguard Stations: Would mainly be required for watch in bad weather or during periods of low visibility and would generally be situated in less important areas, near small fishing ports, etc.

(*d*) Auxiliary Stations: These would provide for the maintenance of bad weather watch in areas where the amount of traffic does not justify the employment of full-time personnel.'

The Committee reported that there were 350 stations of which 252 were Coastguard Stations and ninety-eight auxiliary stations. They proposed that the Coastguard Stations should be reduced to 217 with 142 auxiliary stations making a new total of 359. They agreed with the Board of Trade that the total personnel should be 772, a reduction of 48.

After studying the Auxiliary Coastguard, the Committee recommended the acceptance of a Board of Trade proposal that auxiliary personnel should be enrolled into a Coast Life-saving Corps. 'We consider that the idea of performing some national service connected with the sea, and the saving of life would make such an appeal that in a comparatively short time a large body of qualified voluntary helpers would be available to assist the Coastguard Service. A Coast Life-saving Corps would become an important national asset developing an *esprit de corps* of its own', the Committee declared.

The Report then vindicated the Coastguard Service and sought to allay public concern. 'It has not been established that any failure has occurred for which the service could be held responsible.

'In the case of the *Islander,* the Board of Trade accept the view that there was a failure in local administration. In any large organization failures, mainly on account of the human factor, must unfortunately be expected to occur from time to time, but such failures do not necessarily reflect upon its efficiency as a whole. Considerable publicity has been given to the case of the *Islander,* and we feel that if equal publicity had been given to the many valuable services which have been performed by the Coastguard, no question of its general efficiency would have arisen.

'Before 1923 Coastguardsmen frequently patrolled the coast in fine weather for revenue protection duties and were much in evidence, but under existing conditions the bulk of the work of the Service is performed at look-out huts in bad weather. Their absence does not mean that the service has become less efficient, on the contrary we are satisfied that the reverse is the case'.

One more storm had been weathered by H.M. Coastguard.

12
To War Again

The recommendations of the 1931 Committee were gradually implemented and resulted in the number of Coastguard Districts being reduced from forty-nine to forty-two, and the regular personnel from 820 to the proposed 772.

Further adjustments were made from time to time and, at the start of World War II there were 204 stations manned by 719 regular coastguards. Sixty-five were Constant Watch Stations, fifty-seven Constant Night Watch and eighty-two Occasional Watch Stations.

In addition there were 176 auxiliary stations of which ninety-two kept regular watch during bad and thick weather.

The vindication of the Coastguard Service by the Committee greatly strengthened morale but the Chief Inspector in his Report for 1931 issued a word of caution.

'There is a general realization that as a life-saving service H.M. Coastguard is in its youth, and that there is no excuse for resting on oars with the consequent risk of drifting. A body whose primary function is life-saving must keep abreast of the times, must constantly be considering what improvements in methods and organization are necessary, consistent with due economy, and above all it must guard sedulously against any tendency to slacken in the first requirement – a vigilant look-out'.

The Chief Inspector recognized that the enemy of the Coastguard was monotony on the quieter parts of the coast, and that a very high degree of conscientiousness was necessary on the part of men who night after night were required to maintain watch by themselves, in a darkened hut, often in a very isolated position, if they were to maintain unceasing vigilance. It was necessary to guard against the attention wandering even momentarily as it was possible that at that moment mariners in peril might burn an inefficient signal of distress which might be their last one. Next morning bodies and wreckage might be washed up on the beach.

With the growth of civil aviation an extensive organization for dealing with possible crashes in the North Sea and English Channel was set up in 1933, with the Coastguard as the linchpin. The area involved was bounded by a line from Naze to Rotterdam, and Beachy Head to Boulogne. If a radio message was received at Lympne that an aircraft was in difficulties the information was passed to Sandgate Coastguard Station which became the controlling station for shore-based rescue operations.

If an aircraft was going down in the sea her position was obtained by directional bearings, by Lympne, and was plotted on a specially designed chart at Sandgate, which showed at a glance which lifeboats were best placed to afford immediate assistance.

Regular exercises were held and the system, which included the use of twelve lifeboats, was reported to function rapidly and smoothly.

Already in 1930 plans had been made to involve the Coastguard in the Observer Corps organization for spotting enemy aircraft in wartime, but Observer Corps exercises held during that year showed that although the Coastguards and men of the Naval War Signal Stations co-operated when they could, in practice they would be unable to take any effective or active part in the organization in the first twenty-four hours of war because of their other duties.

It was therefore decided that the Observer Corps should man the coastal observer posts from the commencement of 'Air Defence Look-out', and this eliminated the Coastguard and naval personnel from active participation, except in areas not watched by the Corps.

The nature of the general duties of the Coastguard gradually changed in the 1930s and, in 1935 the summer months were reported to be affording the Life-saving Service a period of considerable activity. Casualties to large vessels requiring direct action by the L.S.A. Companies were becoming less frequent due to the modern aids to navigation which were available, but casualties to small craft, especially yachts with unskilled amateur crews, and fishing boats with motors broken down, occurred with great suddenness and if life was to be saved, demanded the utmost promptness in sending the appropriate assistance.

The tendency was for rescues to be made by lifeboats under conditions in which, in the past, the L.S.A. Companies would have been relied upon. This was mainly due to the replacement of the old types of rowed and sailing lifeboats by modern high-powered motor lifeboats which could operate effectively in sea and weather conditions which the older types could not have faced.

The L.S.A. Companies were ancillary to the lifeboat and were normally employed only when the lifeboat could not operate, but when they were called out it was usually in very difficult conditions which required skill and professional knowledge of a very high order.

'The lifeboat service being a voluntary one, supported by public subscription, has gripped the imagination of the masses, but it must not be forgotten that behind the launch of every lifeboat there is an organization, the whole object of which is to ensure that in the event of a vessel being seen or reported to be in distress, appropriate assistance is summoned without delay', wrote the Chief Inspector in 1936. 'We consider that in fairness to the look-out and intelligence duties of H.M. Coastguard and the Coast Life-saving Corps this should be appreciated'.

Another reason for the reduction in calls for the services of the L.S.A. Companies was the efficiency of the Coastguard warning system to vessels standing into danger which had been greatly increased. A large percentage of the vessels warned would in the past have become casualties calling for rescue by the Companies.

In 1938 the Admiralty decided that if war came they would not use their powers under the 1925 Coastguard Act to take over the administration and control of the Coastguard. The Board of Trade was requested to be responsible for the force when the Coastguard became a War Watching Organization, as well as a life-saving service.

Arrangements were consolidated for the transition from a peace to a war emergency organization with the minimum disturbance, and it was planned that the role of the Coastguard could be changed within one hour of the order being given.

The Admiralty stressed the great importance of signalling knowledge by the Coastguard and arrangements were made for signalling practices between H.M. Ships and the Stations. The Admiralty reported that the standard of signalling was high.

There were, of course, a number of ex-naval signallers in the Coastguard but the bulk of the remainder were trained after they joined the Service.

In 1937 the plans for the War Watching Organization were finalized. The basis of the organization was the maintenance of look-out by the personnel of the Coastguard Stations, War and Port War Signal Stations round the coasts, to enable warning to be given of the approach of enemy forces or other dangers so that defensive action could be taken.

The Stations were to continue to perform their normal peace-time duties, subordinating them as might be necessary to the more urgent War Watching duties. In addition to their function as part of the War Watching Organization certain stations were called upon to function as part of the Air Intelligence Organization, reporting the movements of enemy aircraft.

The coasts of Great Britain and Ireland were divided into Commands, each under the appropriate Commander-in-Chief. Scotland from the border on the east coast to Bennane Head on the west coast, ten miles north of Loch Ryan.

The Nore – from the Scottish border at Berwick upon Tweed to the south coast.

Portsmouth – the south coast.

Plymouth – the south coast to Bennane Head and the coast of Ireland.

The Board of Trade reported to the Admiralty on the state of the Coastguard in a letter dated 4th June 1937.

There were twelve Inspectors, forty-one District Officers, 155 Station Officers and 522 Coastguardsmen. In addition 900 Auxiliary Watchers had been enrolled in the Coast Life-saving Corps. Of these approximately 500 were attached to Coastguard Stations and were employed as reliefs when necessary during prolonged periods of bad weather and, when the complement of a Coastguard Station was below establishment. The remaining 400 Auxiliary Watchers were attached to Auxiliary Stations where watch was set in varying degrees of bad and thick weather.

Of the 500 Auxiliaries attached to Coastguard Stations forty-one were of military age – eighteen–twenty-five years – and of the 400 attached to Auxiliary Stations twenty-four were in this age-group. It was likely that the proportion of men of military age would decrease as the number of watchers enrolled in the

Corps was considerably increased about five years earlier, and a large number of these men might be expected to continue in the Corps until they reached the age of sixty or sixty-five.

About twelve per cent of the Coastguard personnel were ex-R.N. signal or telegraphy ratings and these men had reached a considerably higher standard of signalling than was required in the Coastguard, but except for those who had recently left the naval service some refresher training in naval procedures would probably be required.

The Auxiliaries were recruited from varied occupations including mining, fishing and agriculture and included a fair proportion of older men.

The examinations and tests for the Coastguard required skill in semaphore and morse, up to ten words a minute flashing and eight words a minute by flag waving. They also needed perfect knowledge of general distress signals and a thorough knowledge of all signals made to and from lifeboats. Knowledge of regulations for preventing collisions, and special signals for Coastguard duties – the ability to indicate to a vessel that she was standing into danger in clear and thick weather by day and night.

At an informal meeting between the Board of Trade and the Admiralty on 24th May 1938 the Board pointed out that the type of Coastguard employed by them could not be expected to undertake any very elaborate duties or accept any very considerable degree of responsibility. It would be necessary for instructions to be simple and concise.

The Board of Trade prepared secret instructions for Inspectors and District Officers at the end of May 1939 when the danger of war loomed. These instructions were to be put into operation at a moment's notice by a code telegram, and a request was made for fifty-three steel boxes for these officers, to keep the papers safe.

A covering letter with the instructions, headed H.M. Coastguard War Watching Organization – Secret, told the senior officers that the organization had now been so far developed as to enable instructions to be issued regarding the first action of the Coastguard in an emergency.

'These instructions are contained in the enclosed Secret envelope which is not to be opened unless a special order to do so is given. This order will be sent by telegram as follows:

To Inspector – or District Officer . . . "Guardian" from "Shipminder". The code word Guardian has been inserted on the secret envelope to indicate that it is the envelope to be opened on receipt of the telegram. You are requested to acknowledge the safe receipt of the secret envelope and, pending the supply of steel boxes, arrangements should be made for the safe custody of the papers under lock and key'.

The 'secret' instructions were that on receipt of the coded telegram 'Guardian' from the Board of Trade all Coastguard Stations were to be placed on constant watch, using supplementary watchers if necessary, and were to report suspicious vessels including any warship whether thought to be British or foreign, and any other ship which was either of a type not normally seen in the area, or which appeared to be acting in an unusual manner such as dropping articles overboard, or steaming slowly for a considerable period.

The proposed 'secret' instructions and covering letter were shown to the Admiralty and approval was given for their issue. The Admiralty were not however impressed by the cloak and dagger method of circulation suggested. 'We feel that the present lull in the international situation affords an excellent opportunity for issuing the instructions. We also feel that it is unnecessary to circulate them in sealed secret envelopes. There is nothing secret or really confidential in the memorandum and furthermore there is every reason for Inspectors and District Officers to be able to study it in peace, so as to make the necessary arrangements for transmission of messages etc. in advance. For the same reason we also feel that it is not necessary to issue tin boxes specially for the custody of the memorandum. The only real point to avoid is conveying the impression that the Government fear an early outbreak of war.

'We therefore suggest that the memorandum should be sent now, marked "Confidential" but with a cautionary note that it is necessary to avoid giving undue publicity to the matter.'

The Coastguard took part in a Coast Defence exercise during July of 1938 and the Admiralty reported only one criticism of their work. This was in their identification and recognition of naval craft but in this they had had little practice, and one lesson from the exercise was the necessity of special training in the subject being given to all personnel earmarked for war watching duties. It was proposed that copies of silhouettes of British, French and German men-o'-war should be supplied to all Coastguard Stations on the east and south coasts.

When war came the Admiralty did not exercise their powers under the Coastguard Act 1925, and the Service remained within the control of the Board of Trade until the Marine Division of the Board was transferred to the Ministry of Shipping.

Throughout the early months of 1939 the Admiralty and the Board of Trade perfected and consolidated the War Watching Organization, and the transfer from peace routine to war was quick and smooth. The newly appointed Naval Authorities found in their Areas a well-equipped and well-trained Intelligence Service already in being.

Great credit was due to the District Officers who accepted the added responsibilities and work.

As the War Organization was modelled on the peacetime service, the Auxiliary Coastguards, as they were called, were recruited from the Watchers in the Coast Life-saving Corps, and were enrolled under the National Service Scheme. They provided the extra personnel which enabled the Coastguard Stations to maintain the more intensive degree of watching necessary under war conditions.

The Coastguards-men quickly proved their worth, and a steady stream of information on incidents at sea and on the coasts was fed back to the various control centres. Not every alert was as sinister as it appeared at first sight.

In April 1940, the Coastguard at Holy Island, off the Northumbrian coast, was informed by a fisherman that two men were taking pictures of Lindisfarne Castle and, that they had been asking if there were any guns on the island.

Police on the mainland were told and ordered that the men be stopped, but they had already left the island in a rowing boat for the mainland. The Coastguard reported this to the police station at Belford, a few miles away, and the men were detained. They proved to be students from Oxford University, but they had their cameras confiscated and the films in them were sent to the security headquarters to be developed.

The freedom from Admiralty control did not survive the early months of the war, and in May 1940, with the prospect of invasion after the retreat from Dunkirk, the Admiralty considered it essential that the Coastguard should be armed, not only for their personal protection but to enable them to take offensive action to safeguard their lines of communication. It was therefore decided to implement Section 2 of the 1925 Act bringing the service under Admiralty control. All personnel were brought under the Naval Discipline Act and were borne on the books of H.M.S. *President II*.

When the German air force attacked, the Coastguards and their stations did not escape the attentions of the enemy. In July 1940 Fowey, Cornwall was bombed and the only bomb which did any damage was one that fell on a school alongside the Polruan Coastguard Station destroying the telephone lines. The Coastguard on watch fired his rifle at the enemy plane which continued to circle at a low altitude. It was claimed locally that the coastguardsman made several hits in spite of being machine-gunned by the enemy.

After control passed to the Admiralty, the First Lord appointed Vice-Admiral R. V. Holt to carry out an inspection of the Coastguard organization. Having toured the Coastguard headquarters and stations in all parts of the country the Admiral reported that he considered it absolutely essential that the service should be attached to one of the operational Divisions of the Admiralty. All the Coastguard work was intimately connected with local defence and from not being in close enough touch misunderstandings had arisen. He submitted that a meeting should be held to consider the transfer of the Coastguard Section of the Admiral Commanding Reserves Office to the operational side of the Admiralty.

The Chief Inspector of Coastguard in his general report for 1940 was critical of the Admiral's inspection. 'As this officer had no special qualifications for the task with which he had been entrusted it cannot be said that the Coastguard Service benefited in any respect as a result of his activities'.

However, the Admiral did discover one unique band of Watchers and reported that north of Dornock there were suitable landing places which could be used by the enemy but these were adequately watched. 'At Golspie there is a Corps of Lady Watchers under the leadership of Miss Alexandra Sinclair who take their duties very seriously. Their reports are excellent and they are thoroughly alert'.

In addition to their war duties the Coastguard and the Life-saving Companies were frequently engaged in rescues from shipwrecks. One of the biggest of such operations occurred on 17th October 1940 when the largest number of people to be rescued at one time were brought ashore by breeches buoy.

Three destroyers en route for the Tyne ran aground on the rocks at Whitburn shortly after midnight. One of the vessels was refloated but the other two H.M.S. *Ashanti* and H.M.S. *Fame* remained hard aground, side by side about 150 yards apart and the *Fame* caught fire.

The Roker and the South Shields Life-saving Brigades were called out and the South Shields Brigade fired a line over the *Fame*. The sea was covered with escaping oil and cotton waste which fouled the whip and hawser.

Members of the local fire brigade went out in the breeches buoy to help deal with the fire, and about sixty members of the crew were brought ashore. The operation was then halted while ammunition which was in danger of exploding was unloaded, but by dawn 104 men had been rescued by the two brigades from the two destroyers.

A week later the two brigades were back in action when the M/V *Cairngorm* went ashore at Marsden. The 5,000 tons vessel was being towed off the rocks when she broke her back. The noise was heard on shore and, as the weather was worsening, the brigades with the assistance of the army got a line on board and rescued the crew of forty-nine. The following March the two brigades working together rescued the twenty-two man crew of a minesweeper which went ashore on the same rocks.

By 1941 the Naval authorities were beginning to appreciate the value of the Coastguard as a naval intelligence service and a large number of Stations were utilized for a special reporting system which played a major part in the anti-invasion plans of the Government. It was arranged that any signs of a possible enemy landing were to be reported direct to the appropriate military authority and in many stations the military installed field telephones at the look-outs to expedite reports.

Enemy activity was also to be reported by firing specially designed warning rockets and, at some Stations in the north of the country radio telephony sets were installed for the same purpose.

There was very close association with the Royal Observer Corps and 145 direct telephone lines were installed between Coastguard Stations and the Air Observer Posts.

In some areas there was complete dependence on the Coast-guard for air observation, and the Coastguard Headquarters received many gratifying signals from R.A.F. fighter units about the valuable reports from the Coastguard which had led to the destruction of enemy aircraft.

For some time the Coastguard had had local arrangements for assisting in 'security' and these took the form of dawn patrols which were carried out daily to look for footprints and other signs on the beaches which might indicate that an enemy agent had landed.

The Service was told that it was performing valuable war service on the effectiveness of which might depend the success or failure of the general organization to deal with the possible landing of enemy forces on the coasts.

The Chief Inspector commented: 'It is feared that there is a very dim realization, if any, by the general public of their dependence on our Service'.

The war made the work of life-saving much more difficult. The Coastguard were forbidden to fire maroons to call out the L.S.A. Companies or the lifeboat crew. In dealing with a shore rescue there were the hazards of tank traps, barbed wire and landmines to add to the problems always present in this form of rescue. When it was necessary to launch the lifeboat permission had to be sought from the Naval authorities to prevent the lifeboat from running into minefields or other forms of marine defence.

A wartime feature of life-saving was the introduction of the Air/Sea Rescue Service for snatching airmen from ditched planes. This service was inaugurated in 1941 by the Air Ministry and the Admiralty and was controlled operationally by the Naval authorities, but the Coastguard initiated action if casualties were spotted from a look-out.

In the south-eastern division a plan was devised for 'fixing' an airman baling-out by cross-bearings from Coastguard Look-outs. This enabled a bearing to be given to the 'crash boats' as the air/sea rescue launches were known. They could then locate the casualty without delay, and this was important in winter.

The wartime organization of the Coastguard was:

Chief Inspector who was located at the Ministry of War Transport.

Deputy Chief Inspector attached to Admiral Commanding Reserves, Admiralty.

Twelve Inspectors with the rank of Captain R.N. in charge of Coastguard Divisions.

One Sub-Inspector, rank Lieutenant Commander and forty-four District Officers, rank Lieutenant R.N. in charge of Coastguard Districts.

There were three to five Districts in each Division and the personnel totalled 650 regular Station Officers and Coastguardsmen and 4,500 Auxiliary Coastguardsmen enrolled locally and trained for War Watching duties in their own locality.

In addition, in certain more remote parts of the coast a Coast Searcher was enrolled whose duties were to keep an occasional look-out and report happenings of interest.

All regular Coastguards and the majority of the Auxiliary Coastguards were armed with rifles for the protection of their look-outs and communications. A Defence Regulation had constituted the auxiliary personnel as Armed Forces of the Crown who were subject to naval discipline while on duty.

From 16th February 1942, at the request of the Admiralty, they were dressed in khaki battledress, and as battledress became available the regulars were also kitted out with it instead of their naval-type reefer jackets. Their seafaring background was maintained by the retention of the blue-peaked cap with the Coastguard badge.

Although some of the older men deplored the loss of the traditional blue uniform the change was reported to be highly popular throughout the service. The men took a pride in their appearance and the Coastguard as an armed and disciplined service compared very favourably with other branches of the armed forces of the Crown.

Sten-guns had come into general use and each man in the Coastguard was armed with a rifle or sten. Some look-out huts also had Thompson sub-machine guns issued.

In 1941 several Coastguard stations suffered damage from

enemy bombing and one, on the south coast, received a direct hit from an enemy gun fired from the French coast. In very many cases the look-out huts were blasted by machine-gun fire from the air. But in spite of the large number of incidents there were no fatal casualties among the regular Coastguards although some members of their families and some auxiliary coastguards were killed.

As 'D-Day' approached warnings went out to the Coastguard Stations that the enemy might attempt to land individual spies or saboteurs disguised in British, American or other Allied uniforms, or even parties of men using captured British landing-craft. They were also reminded that it was important to report the sighting of carrier pigeons. Those flying outward from the coast were especially important as they might be dispatched by enemy agents, but the Coastguards were warned that on no account were pigeons to be shot.

The Northern Ireland Coastguards were alerted to watch for illegal landings by the I.R.A. who, it was thought, might attempt to land a small armed party on a lonely part of the coast.

The incidence of 'D-Day' and Allied superiority in the air greatly reduced the vital importance of the Coastguard. The prospect of invasion had disappeared, and the possibility of raids by airborne troops was negligible, but the country was subjected to intensive attack by flying-bombs. It was an Auxiliary Coastguard Station in the south-east which reported a flying-bomb as such, using the codeword, at 04.05 on 13th June 1944, probably one of the first bombs to be launched against this country.

Coastguard Stations on the Kent coast were subjected to heavy gun-fire from the French coast until the end of September 1944.

It was decided that a War Watch on the coast must be maintained but with a lower degree of intensity, and the Coastguard organization was therefore modified in 1944, with extensive reductions in staff. The number of Auxiliary Coastguards went down from the 1942 peak of 5,215 to 3,191.

By the end of 1944 the post-war organization was receiving close attention both at the Admiralty and the Ministry of War Transport, which had taken over from the Ministry of Shipping.

The Chief Inspector drew attention to the new services of great importance which had come into being during the war in the life-saving field. Air/sea rescue, the Royal Observer Corps and radar in particular. He considered that the first two would need some counterpart in the post-war world, and radar, when no longer restricted to military use, might be expected to be an important factor in any system of coast intelligence.

Having heard rumours of a possible 'take-over bid' the Chief Inspector was scathing: 'It is unfortunate that there are to be found in the Admiralty a certain number of naval officers now holding minor administrative posts who, without giving the question mature thought, are voicing the opinion that on the conclusion of hostilities the Coastguard should not be 'given back' to this Department'. Actually the Service has never been fully controlled by the Admiralty and this is not realized by those referred to. Further, they do not realize that in wartime the Coastguard does not serve the Royal Navy exclusively, but also the armed forces serving under the War Office and Air Ministry.

'Also they are not aware that in peacetime the Coastguard performs no duties for any of the fighting services, and its control by the Admiralty would be quite illogical.

'In the past, when under the Admiralty, little interest was taken in the Service by that Department. There was no incentive to zeal, and no scope for initiative and resource, and the only useful function of the Coastguard in those days appeared to be to provide jobs for those temporarily without them.

'During the last twenty-two years the Coastguard has given loyal and faithful service to this Department. It has built up a tradition of its own, and there is an *esprit-de-corps* which is a distinctive feature of the modern Coastguard.

'It is urged strongly that this Department safeguards the future welfare and efficiency of the Service by retaining administrative control, and opposing any legislation which might lead to the adoption of control by the Admiralty'.

The Ministry of War Transport wrote to the Admiralty in December 1944, asking for the return of the Coastguard and this provoked a minor 'paper war'.

The Head of Military Branch at the Admiralty commenting on the request in a Minute declared that 'The only alternative would be to settle now whether we intend to stake out a definite claim to permanent control. Since such a claim would clearly meet with severe opposition and since we should need a well-defined case to stand any chance of success, it is suggested that it would be better if possible to defer the settlement of Admiralty policy on this point until we can see more clearly what the post-war future is likely to be'.

The Director of Local Defence concurred that it would be unwise to make a definite answer. 'At the same time it is considered that the situation in which we found ourselves in 1939 and 1940 was very unsatisfactory and steps should be taken to avoid any recurrence of such a dilemma. The writer of this Minute was associated with all the difficulties which arose and there is no doubt that the security of the coast was much impaired for many months in this way.

'While the Coastguard Act of 1925 has not been closely studied it is considered that it is a bad Act in its elementary principles because:

(a) So far as can be ascertained it had and has no advantage or avowed object except to satisfy disarmament cranks by transferring the financial cost of the Coastguard from the Naval Estimates to less contentious 'Shipping Estimates'.

(b) It directly causes the operation, administration, location and even strength of the Coastguard Service to be absolutely divorced from any considerations of the military guarding of the coasts or even Naval War Plans.

(c) It is apparent that the Coastguard properly handled is a valuable naval reserve. If we had had it in our hands at full strength before the war it would have provided the parent for many odd parties which had to be raised on 'ad hoc' lines e.g. Mine Watchers, Clyde River Patrol, Naval Home Guard Sections. The work of the U.S. Coastguard Service alone shows what can be done if such is required.

(d) The Force becomes entirely unmilitary in general character even to the extent of being unable safely to handle small-arms without training.

'It doubtless does valuable civilian work such as life-saving duties, ship reporting, shore encroachment prevention, shore salvage and wreck reporting, but it could do those as well or better if it remained under the Admiralty.

'In the Director of Local Defence's opinion the desirability and even plain practicability of returning to the Coastguard Act, 1925, should be called into question by the Admiralty before any final arrangements are concluded'.

This Minute fell into the hands of the Chief Inspector of Coastguard a week later, and he was moved to write a Minute: 'The Minute of the Director of Local Defence contains serious allegations respecting the administration and the efficiency of H.M. Coastguard which cannot pass unchallenged.

'Grave exception is taken to the statement that the "security of the coast was much impaired for many months". The question of implementing Section 2 of the Coastguard Act was very fully considered both before and after the outbreak of hostilities, and it was decided that this step was unnecessary as the organization arranged with the Admiralty fully met the needs of the war situation. There is no evidence on record to the contrary, and naval authorities on the coast were fully satisfied'.

Early in 1945 the Ministry of War Transport received a letter from the Admiralty which seemed to suggest that the Navy would like to keep the Coastguard after the war.

In an internal Minute, the Ministry declared: 'We should not accept the position in the Admiralty letter. That letter suggests that the Admiralty control of the Coastguard should continue at least until the end of the Japanese war, if only for reasons of military security. It implies the possibility of the Coastguard remaining after the war under the control of the Admiralty and this could not be contemplated. We should get this matter thrashed out at once.

'In the years following on 1923 there was a vast improvement made in the life-saving organization because we had actual control of the Coastguard, and could make it a real life-saving organization.

'We are already engaged in considering changes that will have to be made in the life-saving organization after the war, and we must be sure that the Coastguard returns to us.

'We should at once counter the implied suggestion in the Admiralty letter that they may keep the Coastguard, for there will be a body of opinion there in favour of keeping the Coastguard, merely because it is useful to have a body to which R.N. officers and ratings, not required for naval purposes, can be posted'.

F*

The Ministry wrote to the Admiralty, and their representations resulted in a further letter from the Admiralty that a decision had been reached that the Coastguard was to revert to the control of the Ministry.

The Ministry asked that the service should revert to the blue uniform, and the Admiralty, agreeing to this, hoped that in future recruitment to the regular service would be restricted to ex-naval officers and men. The Ministry made no firm commitment, merely stating that the Admiralty recommendation had been noted.

In September 1945, a message went out from Coastguard Headquarters to the Force, informing it that the transfer of control would mean that the Auxiliary Coastguard would be disbanded, and that Supplementary Watchers of the Coast Lifesaving Corps would have to be relied upon to keep watch at Auxiliary Stations, and, to act as reliefs at other Coastguard Stations.

The Service reverted to the control of the Ministry of War Transport on 1st October 1945, and the Admiralty was informed that the Coastguard could not depart from the policy adopted for many years that, whilst the fullest consideration was given to ex-naval officers and men, officers and men of the Merchant navy were equally eligible for appointment.

The Auxiliary Coastguard was disbanded on 30th November 1945.

The stage was set for development as the great life-saving service of modern times.

13
The Modern Coastguard Service

The Admiralty gave up control in 1945, but it was to be a further nineteen years before the Coastguard returned to the Marine Division of the Board of Trade.

When the Ministry of War Transport became the Ministry of Transport, and later the Ministry of Transport and Civil Aviation, the Coastguard continued to be administered by the Ministry. Every effort was made to maintain the pre-war system of coast-watching, and the life-saving apparatus continued to be manned by the Companies of the Life-saving Corps.

The duties of the Coastguard were to keep a look-out for vessels or aircraft in distress, danger or difficulties, and to render assistance directly by using the life-saving appliances, or indirectly by informing the lifeboat, air traffic control and other authorities who could render assistance.

The coast-watching system was based on visual watch from 314 look-out huts sited on headlands or other vantage points, with the huts five miles apart where small ship traffic was heavy and ran close to the coast, but a greater distance apart where danger was less.

The normal type of watch was 'bad weather' and apart from occasional scanning of the coast and sea by day, constant watch was only kept at points where there was a large volume of small coastal and fishing-boat traffic and, where the navigational hazards were such that immediate action was necessary to save lives if a casualty occurred even in fine weather.

A night watch was kept in fine weather at a sufficient number of stations to ensure that watch was set at all other stations on the approach of bad weather.

In addition, a constant listening watch was kept on the marine distress waves by ten Coast Radio Stations of the Post Office. Any distress messages received were immediately passed by telephone to the nearest Coastguard Station which initiated all rescue measures.

The Coastguard Station crews were recruited from pensioners of the Royal Navy and men of the Merchant Navy with equivalent sea service.

With the ending of the war there were plenty of volunteers to join the Coastguard, and the Service could afford to be selective. It was soon clear that the new men, although naval pensioners, were of a considerably higher standard than some of the pre-war personnel who, in a number of areas, had given the civil population a misleading impression of the service. People talked of hard drinking old salts whose children ran barefoot while they frittered away their pensions in the local taverns. It took several years before this unfortunate image was dispelled.

The Ministry continued the award of the Life-saving Shield for the best wreck service, and started a rebuilding programme to provide better homes for coastguardsmen and their families.

Modern equipment was installed in the Coastguard Stations – innovations which were urgently needed as Coastguardsman G. A. Black of Gorleston pointed out in a letter to the *Coastguard Magazine* in 1967.

'What a change in the Coastguard service in the past thirty years. Today we have all "mod. cons", indoor toilets with H & C laid on, electric lights everywhere, electric ovens, washing machines, refrigerators, radiators, R/T, up-to-date 10-inch Signalling Projectors – the lot. About the only thing we haven't got at the moment is an electric gadget to prime, place and fire the maroons.

'It's a "piece of cake" compared with the old days of paraffin lamps and oil stoves in the look-out. It used to take ages to boil a kettle for a "cuppa" at New Brighton, where there was even a paraffin lamp on the living-room table – it was a common occurrence to find oneself eating "paraffin butter" because of an overflow or a leak.

'In those days when the lifeboat left her moorings the stand-by man had to run down to a convenient spot and pass the position of the casualty, the course to steer and any other information by semaphore. It wasn't much of a picnic in a blizzard standing on the top of the old Perch Rock Battery making and reading semaphore'.

One of the most important improvements in equipment made immediately after the war was the introduction of the cordite Rescue Rocket to replace the Boxer Rocket. The new rocket was first used at a wreck service on the Northumbrian coast on 31st January 1950.

This was the biggest single casualty in that year, when the coaster *Rask* went aground off Saltpanhoe Beach, a few miles south of Berwick upon Tweed. Fourteen members of the crew and one passenger were brought safely ashore after an eleven-hour struggle in the teeth of a gale. In the following New Year's Honours List District Officer George Heppel was awarded the M.B.E.

Soon after 6 a.m. the *Rask* was ploughing through mountain-ous seas a few hundred yards from the shore. Registered at Hau Gesund, Norway, the coaster of 631 tons was bound for New-castle with a cargo of herrings from Bergen. The gale was driving sleet towards the shore and visibility varied from a few hundred yards to nil, with squalls reaching eighty miles an hour.

Though originally designed as a mine-sweeper towards the end of the first World War, the *Rask* had been refitted and con-verted into a motor-ship only eighteen months previously. She carried a radio-telephone, radar and direction-finding apparatus. The Chief Officer was on the bridge and thought that she was fifty miles north of her actual position because the weather had made accurate observations impossible. She ran aground, the well-deck was flooded and thirty-foot waves crashed over the gunwales, she had a forty-five degree list. As dawn broke the crew saw that she was lying 400 yards off the coast, broadside on. The siren blasted the S.O.S. which was heard two miles inland. The signalman at Scremerston railway station saw through a break in the snow the light of a ship about a mile away, further inshore than he had ever seen a vessel before. He reported to his head-quarters and the Coastguard at Berwick was telephoned by British Rail controller, Newcastle who informed the duty look-out that a ship appeared to be ashore.

This was at 7.32 a.m. The District Officer called out the Berwick lifeboat and the L.S.A. Company.

The lifeboat reached the scene in about thirty minutes, but could not get in close enough to effect a rescue. She turned back but could not get into Berwick and had to sail sixteen miles north to Dunbar where she was helped back into harbour by the Dunbar lifeboat.

The tide was flooding, the gale still blowing with rain and snow squalls and District Officer Heppel estimated visibility at about one mile. The shore was flat and sandy with tongues of rock on one of which the *Rask* was aground, about 400 yards out.

Never had a rescue been effected by breechs buoy from such a distance. To shorten the shot Mr Heppel ordered the company to set up the projector on a rocky outcrop twenty-five yards out in the surf. As the waves pounded in the men were drenched to their waists.

When the rocket is prepared for firing, the wire trace and spring are laid in three wide zigzags in front of the projector. The line-box is placed behind them. On the right is the whip box, according to the drill-book.

The crew set up the equipment and the first roller swept everything back to the beach.

The District Officer ordered the apparatus to be set up again and this time two men were detailed to sit on the line-box two on the whip-box and he held on to the projector.

Between waves the rocket was aimed at the wreck. 'Fire!' shouted Mr Heppel, the No. 1 pressed the firing key slung round his neck. Nothing happened. Sand and salt water had worked between the contacts. The contacts were removed, rubbed with emery-cloth, and as each piece was cleaned, it was wrapped in a handkerchief to keep it dry. The firing procedure was carried out again and there was another misfire, followed by yet another.

At the fourth attempt the rocket soared away into the gale and shot straight to the target at 360 m.p.h. Some way beyond the *Rask* the rocket plunged into the sea laying the line across the bows. The crew were in the wheelhouse and before they could reach it the line was swept off into the sea.

Another rocket was fired and the line fell between the masts – contact had been made within ten minutes of the arrival of the life-saving company.

After securing the line the crew started to haul out the whip to which was attached the pulley-block buoyed by a fisherman's float. As it was only 250 yards long, Station Officer W. C. Bowen spliced in the rocket-line which doubled the length. A strong cross-tide carried the whip northwards where it was in danger of fouling the rocks.

Mr Heppel ordered the crew to move northwards along the sandhills to gain height and keep the line as straight as possible. This meant that the line was still too short so a further length of rocket-line was spliced in.

The nine-foot high tripod known as the triangle was set up fifty yards out in the surf to keep the whip as high above the breakers as possible and the breeches buoy was sent out to the ship.

The first man was being brought ashore and three members of the company waded out to meet him when they noticed that a strand of the whip was frayed, it parted and the survivor was dropped into the boiling sea. One of the rescuers was knocked unconscious.

Both men were dragged ashore. A new whip was sent out to the ship but it snagged on the rocks and was irretrievably stuck.

The Life-saving Company from Seahouses then arrived with their whip which was spliced in and the final rescue was successfully completed – at 7.30 p.m. twelve hours after the warning call was received.

The magnificent work of the Coastguard Cliff-Rescue teams provides spectacular stories every summer.

Not every story has a happy ending. Wherever there are high cliffs there are adventurous boys whose search for seabirds' eggs can end in tragedy.

Coastguard reports show two such incidents in 1958. The first was at Stout Bay, a well-known beauty spot at Llantwit Major, in the Vale of Glamorgan.

A fourteen year old Cardiff boy went with a ten year old companion to look for gulls eggs and seeing a nest on the cliff face the elder boy climbed down. When he did not return the younger boy looked over the cliff and saw his friend lying on the beach 150 feet below.

The Coastguard was called out and Coastguardsman E. C. Bailey went down the cliff face and found the boy dead. The cliff was crumbling and although a rope ladder was rigged, Coastguardsman Bailey had to use a line to scramble and slide down the last thirty feet.

The Barry Dock lifeboat made three unsuccessful attempts to land a small boat and it was decided to take the body up the cliff. Station Officer R. J. Peach joined Mr Bailey on the beach and the body was placed in a stretcher. It took two hours' work by the L.S.A. Company to haul the stretcher to the top of the cliff after it frequently snagged on the ragged rocks of the cliff face.

A few days later another boy aged fifteen and a half years was killed when he fell over a cliff at Peel Hill. The Coastguard found him jammed between two rock crevices.

Two incidents with happier endings occurred in the same area a few days later.

A thirteen year old boy slipped and crashed sixty feet onto the jagged rocks between Butter Hole and Port Nissen. The Coastguard team hauled him unconscious up the cliff and he recovered in hospital.

A ten year old Brixham boy climbing on Barry Head was soon trapped on a ledge half-way down a 200 feet high cliff. The Coastguard rescue team were called out.

When Station Officer C. H. Johnson reached the boy he found him suffering from cold and cramp and unable to straighten his arms. The boy and his rescuer were lowered into a dinghy as there was no beach at the bottom of the cliff.

Perhaps the most famous cliff rescuer in the Coastguard Service is known as 'Mr Yo-yo' to the inhabitants of Lulworth. He is Volunteer-in-Charge of the Cliff-Rescue Company, Mr G. A. Plant who was awarded the M.B.E. and bar, for his work. So frequent were his rescue trips up and down the cliffs in the Lulworth area that in the late 1960s the Coastguard Reports tended to cover the incidents with few words 'Our cliff Yo-yo is having another busy season around Lulworth'.

On the East Coast special cliff-rescue parties were formed at Bempton and Flamborough Head. The members, very expert climbers used to collect seabirds' eggs from ledges on the cliffs, using their own specially devised harnesses and gear, until this was prohibited by the protection of various species of birds.

The idea of using the services of these experts in the Coastguard originated with Capt. R. Ramsbottom O.B.E. when he was Inspector of the Yorkshire and Lancashire Division in 1935, but the Bempton Company was not formed until 1946 and the Flamborough Head Company in 1957.

Not only adventurous small boys are rescued by the cliff teams. Frequent calls are received from farmers asking for help to recover sheep which have fallen or jumped off cliffs. One such incident comes from the Isle of Man Coastguard Records.

On 26th July 1957 a request was received from a farmer living about seven miles from Ramsey for assistance in rescuing his sheep which had become stranded on a ledge about fifty feet from the top of the cliff and with nothing but fresh air for 100 feet below. Coastguardsmen Williams, Rayner and Corkish set off by car, and were welcomed on arrival by the grateful farmer, who took them to the cliff-top from where they could look down and get the actual position of the stranded animal. What they saw was not one or two sheep as they expected but thirty-seven terrified beasts packed tightly together on the ledge and, fourteen others, all dead, on the beach below. The slightest scare might result in more being pushed to their doom.

'Some tricky work was needed. First a channel was dug through the clay of the cliff edge and it was through this channel that most of the sheep were eventually hauled to safety. It was 'the bit in between' that was really difficult, but lots of patience and much skilful manoeuvring by the Coastguardsmen and the farmer secured all except two of the thirty-seven sheep who were brought to safety. The other two could not be prevented from jumping to their deaths.'

Life in the modern Coastguard is not without its humorous moments such as the time when a fifty-five year old woman got into difficulties while swimming off a North Wales beach. She was rescued and carried ashore unconscious. There the Coastguard gave her the 'kiss of life'. The woman quickly recovered consciousness, opened her eyes, and slapped her rescuer's face. 'How dare you?' she gasped.

As the work of the Service becomes more widely known, more people telephone the Coastguard Stations seeking information and some strange requests are received.

In 1970 one station on the South Coast was asked by an indignant woman why the red danger flag was always flying at Rottingdean when she wanted to go swimming. She concluded her complaint, 'and I haven't seen any of your men patrolling the beach on horseback this year.'

The same station had a call from a man asking what time was low water. The duty Coastguard replied, '4.30 a.m., Sir'. 'Oh' said the man, 'can you make it a bit later, its rather early for the children.'

Although the introduction of sophisticated navigational aids has reduced the danger to ships of running aground, the work of the Coastguard greatly increased with the boom in week-end sailing since the early 1960s. This type of casualty produced its own rescue service with the introduction by the R.N.L.I. of the Inshore Rescue Boat.

These are fifteen-foot inflatable rubber craft with powerful outboard engines and have a remarkable turn of speed. The boats skim the waves and can safely launch in twenty-foot seas. Each is crewed by a dozen volunteers, usually enthusiasts from the local yacht and sailing clubs, who are on stand-by call in pairs each week from Easter to October.

Some of the boats are equipped with VHF radio provided by the local Round Table or other organization. The speed with which the IRBs, as they are known, can be launched makes them invaluable for rescue work close inshore where the lifeboat could not sail.

A good example of this was shown by the IRB crew at Berwick upon Tweed in 1970. A fibre-glass cabin cruiser, newly purchased, with the owner and his wife on board sailed from the Yacht Club moorings towards the treacherous river bar, against the advice of the Club members. In heavy seas the craft crossed the bar and was immediately struck by a series of huge seas, turned sideways to the waves and overturned.

Two members of the IRB crew launched their craft within four minutes and sped to the spot. They rescued the couple who had no life-jackets on board – the wife was unable to swim – as they clung to the upturned hull.

Spectacular rescues by the Life-saving Companies still take place when gales blow coastal vessels and fishing boats ashore. One of the most thrilling of all time was the snatching of six Dieppe fishermen from the wreck of the trawler *Jeanne Gougy* off Land's End on Saturday 3rd November 1963.

For nearly seven hours the trawler had lain on her side

on the rocks, submerged every few minutes by tremendous waves which prevented rescuers from getting on board from the land, sea, or helicopter. Some of the crew had been swept overboard and drowned as they tried to reach the lines fired to them by the Coastguard from the top of the cliff, but most of the eighteen-man crew were still trapped below decks by the twenty-foot breakers.

After six hours, when it seemed impossible that anyone could still be alive, the watching Coastguards saw the movement of an arm and hand in the dimness of the wheelhouse.

Within seconds a call was made to a helicopter which was standing-by on a car park.

The man in the wheelhouse was exhausted, but with super-human effort he hauled out the whip-block and fastened it to the wheelhouse window frame before collapsing.

The helicopter crew were asked to try to take the man off and Flight Sergeant Eric Smith was lowered to the trawler which was still awash. He carried the exhausted man to the life-line which hoisted him to the hovering helicopter.

While this was being done four more members of the crew emerged with dramatic suddenness from the forepeak and, seeing this, the Coastguard quickly hauled back on the breeches buoy, and, by easing both whips, dropped it on the forecastle. The four men were hauled to safety within twenty minutes.

Immediately afterwards the helicopter returned and Sergeant Smith made a second descent and brought out the sixteen year old cabin boy. There were no more survivors.

The rescued men later told how they were trapped when the ship struck before they had time to shut the watertight doors. They stood for seven hours, up to their chests in water, with their heads in on airlock.

The biggest and most spectacular wreck incident in the history of the Coastguard, however, was the grounding of the giant oil tanker *Torrey Canyon* at 09.11 hours on Saturday 18th March 1967 on Seven Stones Reef, between the Isles of Scilly and Land's End.

She was bound for Milford Haven with a cargo of 117,000 tons of Kuwait crude oil, and struck the reef when travelling at about seventeen knots.

Within two hours a Royal Navy helicopter was over the ship

and the threat of oil pollution was seen to be on a scale which had no precedent anywhere in the world.

H.M. Coastguard were to play a leading part in the enormous rescue and anti-pollution operation set up by the Government in the days that followed.

The Official Log of St Just Coastguard Station illustrates the scope of modern coastguard work as the dramatic story unfolded from the moment that Coastguardsman R. Wallis, who was on watch, received a message from Land's End Radio Station at 09.13 reporting a 'Mayday' distress signal from the stricken tanker.

'*Torrey Canyon*, nationality Liberian, Port of Registry, Monrovia, a steam tanker of 61,263 gross tons, position of grounding seven miles NE Scillies, marked by Light-vessel, wind NNW 5–6, clear, visibility 4–5 miles, waves about 8 feet.'

The Coastguard Log reads:

09.13 From Land's End Radio from Liberian tanker *Torrey Canyon*: 'Ashore on Seven Stones. Require immediate assistance.'

09.18 Helicopter alerted.

09.22 Tug *Utrecht* and Dutch ship *Bierum* report they are proceeding ETA two hours.

09.23 Inspector informed.

09.24 Request scramble helicopter.

09.31 Information requested from C-in-C Plymouth as to positions of H.M. Ships nearest Plymouth.

09.37 Pilot at BEA helicopter reported three French crabbers at tanker.

09.40 *Brambleleafe* reported position 170 degrees, 13 miles from *Torrey Canyon*, closing at 13 knots.

09.44 Situation report to C-in-C and helicopter.

09.47 *Torrey Canyon* asked to report nature of cargo. Replied at 10.28 – crude oil. Lloyd's informed of situation.

09.55 Southern Rescue Co-ordination Centre (joint R.A.F. – Navy) reported two helicopters standing-by at Culdrose within five minutes.

09.59 *Brambleleafe* and *Helenus* ETA expected at *Torrey Canyon* 10.40.

10.01 French trawler *Mater Coristi* reported it was impossible to go close to 'T.C.' Not enough water. Petrol pouring out. On receipt of above helicopters were requested to scramble. S.R.C.C. replied that two helicopters had been scrambled ETA approximately 30 minutes. This information was passed to 'T.C.' and St Mary's lifeboat, which had launched at 09.25.

10.10 Coastguard Inspector arrived at St Just.

10.21 St Mary's lifeboat ETA 10.35.

10.43 St Mary's lifeboat approaching casualty.

10.45 Dr Bell, Hon Sec St Mary's lifeboat requested advance warning of any injured persons being brought to St Mary's. 'T.C.' replied no injuries.

10.50 S.R.C.C. reported helicopters had been delayed, now scrambled, requested Coastguard enquire from 'T.C.' whether crew wished to be taken off by helicopter. Reply: Will make enquiries. Helicopters were requested in first instance as a result of interception which led us to believe there was a grave fire risk. Lifeboat now alongside. 'T.C.' replied 11.25 crew do not require to be taken off by helicopters at the moment. S.R.C.C. advised.

10.57 C-in-C Plymouth requested state of sea. Moderate sea heavy swell.

11.03 St Mary's lifeboat reported that 'T.C.' was waiting for two tugs.

11.04 From Land's End Radio at 10.55 'T.C.' requested 'distress' be cancelled for the moment and treated as 'urgency'.

11.25 St Mary's lifeboat reported that vessel is bending badly from bridge forward. C-in-C on being informed replied that an Assessment Officer was being taken out by helicopter.

11.41 *Brambleleafe* reported exact position of casualty as 242.5 degrees 2.4 miles from Seven Stones Lightvessel.

11.55 Information as to position of tugs requested from Land's End Radio. Replied *Wittezee* ETA daybreak; *Utrecht* ETA 11.30; *Atlantic* ETA this evening; *Albatross* ETA 17.00; *Priadaadraga* ETA 15.00.

12.00 *Utrecht* heard calling naval helicopters on 2182 Kcs Land's End Radio were requested to inform *Utrecht* that helicopters are not fitted with MF.

12.16 Intercepted from *Utrecht*: have arrived position of

casualty. Reported by Inspector to Duty Staff Officer with a request for aerial photographs.

12.20 Inspector discussed with Operations Officer Culdrose possible requirements of helicopters. Operations Officer replied that one would be standing-by.

12.47 Information received from Duty Staff Officer, C-in-C Plymouth that Assessment Officer had been instructed to inform captain of 'T.C.' that helicopters would not be able to operate after dark. If he wished to get some of his crew off to do so during daylight. Report of damage: bulkheads 10-18 smashed. One large rock entered ship forward, aft part amidships hard aground. Main pump-room flooded. Rolling and grinding heavily. Master lightening ship by pumping out crude oil. Forecast similar to now but wind backing to SSW.

12.50 St Just District informed of oil being discharged and the possibility of it coming ashore. Local authorities to be informed. District Officers Hartland and Falmouth also advised.

13.02 Tug *Utrecht* reported that two men had been put on board tanker. At 13.35 reported that oil is drifting 180 degrees and expanding covering an area of about four miles. Coastguard St Mary's informed.

14.25 Situation Report requested from St Mary's lifeboat, and, intention of captain as regards crew being taken off. Replied that helicopter had left, no indication with regard to crew. H.M.S. *Barrosa* approaching. *Utrecht* standing by.

14.31 Information received from C-in-C Plymouth that Salvage Officers and Master were attempting to refloat vessel at 20.00. Captain aware that rescue by helicopter unacceptable after 16.00, if necessary will take to boats. Helicopter standing by at Culdrose at 15 minutes notice. Frigate *Barrosa* heading for area and will stand-by to give assistance. Assessment Officer has been winched off ship.

14.40 Hon Secretary Penlee who is also Lloyd's Agent and Dutch Consul indicated that arrangements for accommodation of crew of 'T.C.' had been arranged at St Mary's. This was passed to Land's End Radio to transmit should crew abandon ship.

16.02   St Mary's lifeboat requested to report whether vessel was still discharging or leaking oil, and to indicate direction and extent. Replied still discharging, direction of drift northerly since 13.30, extent unknown.

16.30   B.E.A. helicopter reported southern tip of oil 050 degrees, six miles from St Mary's forming a tail and turning east. Local authorities St Mary's informed.

16.30   Duty Staff Officer reported that helicopter was airborne to plot extent of oil. H.M.S. *Clarebeston* with thirty-six drums of Gammil spray ETA area 22.00, transferring some of the drums to *Barrosa* and both vessels will spray. Requested intentions should vessel be refloated.

16.37   St Mary's lifeboat asked to get intentions should vessel be refloated. Duty Staff Officer required this information so that he could detail a vessel to follow in 'T.C.'s wake spraying Gammil.

16.58   Inspector Lifeboats SW District requested he be informed should St Mary's lifeboat leave casualty.

17.07   Request from Press Officer, Marine Division, Board of Trade to ask 'T.C.' to stop pumping oil. Vessel reported he was not pumping, oil was leaking from ship.

17.40   Situation Report passed to Deputy Chief Inspector by Inspector.

17.57   St Mary's lifeboat reported that *Utrecht* was still trying to get a line on board 'T.C.' which is further down by the head and rolling and grinding quite a bit. Lifeboat continuing to stand-by until she comes clear or crew require taking off. Unable to find out intentions if she does come clear.

20.26   Information from St Mary's lifeboat that vessel was working heavily. *Utrecht* very close to rocks, uncertain whether line had been passed. D.S.O. Plymouth on being informed indicated that aircraft would be plotting extent of oil A.M. Sunday. Tug *Sea Giant* leaving Plymouth with further supply of spray.

21.35   'T.C.' reported situation at 21.15. Water coming in part of foredeck at high water. List about 8 degrees, 6 feet of water in engine room, boilers closed down, unable to use pumps, on emergency power. No attempt being made to refloat tonight. St Mary's lifeboat standing-by.

Tugs *Utrecht, Albatross, Priadaadraga* in attendance. Tug *Stentor* left Avonmouth 17.00 with large compressors.

21.50 Trinity House Vessel *Stella* proceeded to stand-by Seven Stones Lightvessel in case it was necessary to shift her during the night.

All relevant authorities, C-in-C, S.R.C.C., Superintendent Trinity House, Penzance, Receiver of Wreck, Customs, Press Officer Board of Trade, Lloyd's London, Lloyd's Agent, Hon Secretaries R.N.L.I., Primary and alternative Radio Stations, Local Authorities were kept informed throughout.

SECOND DAY

07.40 Coastguard St Mary's reported weather forecast obtained from R.A.F. St Mawgan, wind NW 15-20 knots gusting 35. Low cloud and drizzle at times. Visibility down to 200 yards in fog patches. Cold front moving in.

St Mary's lifeboat reported that ship did not look too good. Starboard foredeck awash.

08.11 St Mary's lifeboat transferring 14 men from 'T.C.' to THV *Stella*.

08.50 In consultation with Duty Staff Officer it was decided in view of deterioration of weather to advise captain of 'T.C.' to get all crew off. This was transmitted to 'T.C.' with the additional information of difficulty of operation of helicopters in high winds.

11.25 C-in-C Plymouth reported that vessel was now listing ten degrees with starboard bow four degrees down and forward decks awash; tidal streams appeared to be having little effect on oil which was drifting generally in SE direction.

11.30 Situation Report passed to Inspector of Lifeboats SW District.

11.32 Weather forecast for Scilly area obtained from Met. Office Plymouth.

11.45 St Mary's lifeboat suggested to master that he and crew come off in view of weather. He replied no. Waiting for air compressors to arrive and intend to remain for time being.

11.47   *Utrecht* reported to have got a line on board but it parted. Sea getting rough.

12.32   'T.C.' requested helicopter assistance, sea too rough for lifeboat.

13.06   St Mary's lifeboat reported that nine had been taken off. One had fallen in water, remainder refused to jump, waiting for helicopter. Culdrose confirmed helicopters had scrambled. Passed to Land's End Radio for 'T.C.' and lifeboat.

13.36   Duty Staff Officer requested we inform 'T.C.' that helicopters would not be available after 17.30. This information was also received from Culdrose requesting captain to give as much warning as possible should he require to be lifted. Captain replied that he did not think he would require helicopter assistance.

13.44   Information requested from 'T.C.' whether all crew including any operators were being taken off. Replied: Captain and three crew and two from *Utrecht* remaining on board. Nine to be taken off.

13.56   Hon Secretary Penlee requested to launch Penlee lifeboat to relieve St Mary's. St Mary's returning with nine rescued on being relieved.

14.00   Penlee lifeboat launched.

16.52   Information from Coastguard St Mary's that nine of the 'T.C.' had been landed by helicopter, one of the nine on board lifeboat suffering shock. Doctor, St Mary's consulted with lifeboat as regard possibility of lifting man off by helicopter but coxswain decided in view of conditions it was not possible.

16.55   Captain 'T.C.' indicated he did not wish to be lifted off.

17.03   Penlee lifeboat relieved St Mary's.

17.32   Conversation with Operations Officer Culdrose re captain 'T.C.' intention to remain on board. Ops Officer replied that although they did not usually keep helicopters at stand-by, every effort would be made should life be endangered.

THIRD DAY

     Routine messages on the movements of tugs, weather forecasts and oil reports were received until

15.00   Captain 'T.C.' stated that he intended to stay on board, working on instructions of owners. He considered there was a 50–50 chance of refloating and was waiting for compressors, and hoping to refloat on tonight's tide. Ten men still on board. He requests we thank lifeboats, helicopters etc. for assistance given.

18.22   B.E.A. helicopter reported no oil on north and west beaches of Scillies; no oil between wreck and Scillies. St Mary's lifeboat reported thin film of oil from wreck to Scillies. Penlee lifeboat reported thick oil up to nine miles east of wreck.

FOURTH DAY

09.28   Coastguard Stations St Just Division instructed to report any sighting of oil or reports of oil on or near the beaches. Local authorities also informed.

09.42   B.E.A. helicopter reported oil eleven miles east Scillies.

10.52   Chief Inspector Lifeboats, gave instructions that lifeboats would not attend present operations whilst weather remains favourable. Launching and stand-by at the specific request of H.M. Coastguard.

11.21   R.M.S. *Scillonian* reported oil two miles north Wolf Rock.

12.16   From Land's End Radio from Seven Stones Light-vessel at 11.13: after-end of tanker now on fire.

12.18   St Mary's lifeboat advised to launch.

12.20   Helicopter requested from Culdrose: reply 'scrambling now'.

12.22   Tug *Titan* requested medical assistance, doctor required by helicopter. Explosion in engine room of tanker. One man wounded. Culdrose informed and St Mary's requested to send doctor in lifeboat.

12.25   S.R.C.C. reported Shackleton airborne from St Mawgan.

12.30   St Mary lifeboat launched, doctor on board.

12.45   *Titan* reported all salvage crew taken off. Doctor on way in helicopter. Requested ambulance and hospitalization on arrival Newlyn ETA 13.45. Bodmin police informed and requested to arrange ambulance etc.

12.56   *Utretcht* asked to confirm whether there is fire on board tanker. Replied 13.03: Cannot see any fire or smoke.

Man has been lowered from helicopter and taken off again. Hoping to put men on board in hour's time.

14.04   *Utrecht* requested to report number taken off by their boat. Replied: five – no injuries.

14.40   Penlee lifeboat launched at 14.30 with blood to meet *Titan*.

14.45   Link call to *Titan* requestiong information. *Titan* replied that all crew and salvage party had been taken off. One man had died, others minor injuries. Doctor on board and captain of tanker.

During the day there were numerous reports of oil. The general drift was to SE with the nearest patch about six miles from Land's End.

FIFTH DAY

Most reports were of oil pollution.

17.46   Falmouth reported oil on Mullion Island.

18.15   All stations St Just District ordered to report any sightings of oil or pollution of beaches and to examine beaches before dark and at first light, reporting to District H.Q. St Just. Also to request Harbour Authorities. Pilots etc. to do the same.

18.48   British ship *Nevasa* reported southerly limit of oil patch now reaching twenty miles from Ile de Bas. French authorities informed by Land's End Radio.

General direction of drift still SE with a tendency for patches to move easterly towards Lizard.

SIXTH DAY

23.01   Broadcast made by C-in-C on oil situation. A very thick patch exists from *Torrey Canyon* five miles long, three miles wide in a south-easterly direction. Smaller patches exist up to forty miles in a SE direction. Area of pollution exists from wreck out to fifty miles and twenty-three miles wide at the base on a NW-SW axis. Northern boundary five miles clear Land's End and Lizard Point.

SEVENTH DAY

21.04   'Mop-Up'. General organization. C-in-C Plymouth in charge. Inshore Task Force at Falmouth. Army force to

187

assist local authorities. Above authorities to be kept informed of all pollution.

Oil Situation: Thick oil patches five miles round Seven Stones extending ten miles to NE. Thick oil exists around Longships to N & S. Large patch extends SE from Seven Stones for thirty miles, five to ten miles wide, two miles clear of Land's End. Small patch two miles SE Lizard.

Reports from H.M. Coastguard Stations: Oil close inshore from Mounts Bay, Penzance to Pendeen Lighthouse. None on beaches.

EIGHTH DAY

00.25 Inspector instructed all stations on watch, South Western Division to report if any oil has reached the beaches.

01.34 C-in-C Plymouth informed there was a possibility of oil observed and smelt off Cape Cornwall drifting ashore.

06.43–
19.45 Numerous reports of oil on the beaches and off the coast. Situation Report passed to Lloyd's of London.

18.25 C-in-C reported attempts to refloat tanker so far unsuccessful. Tugs still trying, three buttoned on, two destroyers standing-by.

Oil Situation: Thick oil five miles round Seven Stones extending six miles NE off shore from Gnennap Head to Godrevy Island. Belt from one to two miles wide.

Mounts Bay entirely covered, large patches centre two miles south Porthleven laying NNW-SSE fifteen miles long, five miles wide. Light patches twenty miles west of St Agnes Head through Seven Stones to line twenty-five miles SSE Lizard.

Coastal Pollution: Light oil Porthleven beach; thick oil on Pedn Vounder beach, Treen; Cape Cornwall and Priests Cove, St Just; off Sennen Cove and beaches Mounts Bay area. Inspector visited all authorities concerned with oil pollution.

NINTH DAY

12.00 Signal from Deputy Chief Inspector regarding good work carried out by H.M. Coastguard.

19.02   Intercepted: From *Utrecht* to H.M.S. *Delight*. Yes, we have seen she will break soon. No persons on board.

19.15   Intercepted: from *Delight* to spraying vessels. *Torrey Canyon* appears to have broken in two. Maximum spraying effort will be required irrespective of weather tomorrow.

Oil Situation: Very thick oil within area from Seven Stones extending twelve miles S & W then twelve miles E. Thick oil patches five to ten miles wide extending twenty-five miles N. Oil varying density extending twenty-five miles SE from three miles S Lizard, width ten miles. Extensive patches thick and thin oil in area Godrevy Light to Newquay extending twenty miles from coast. Area of oil round Seven Stones Reef expected to increase during the night resulting from wreck breaking her back. Coastal pollution: Oil on beaches Gwithian to Lizard with exception of St Ives.

TENTH DAY

07.07   Coastguard St Mary's reported tanker was awash except for f'castle and amidships superstructure and small part of stern. Seas breaking over her.

14.38   Coastguard St Mary's reported that condition of tanker appears to be deteriorating rapidly. Most of after-part now awash. Gap between the two parts widening. Heavy list to port.

17.24   B.E.A. helicopter pilot reported considerable movement on after-part of tanker. Should she break adrift Seven Stones Lightvessel is directly down wind. Supt Trinity House informed T.H.V. *Stella* sailed to stand-by lightvessel.

Oil Situation: Oil in varying densities now extending from close E of the Scillies to Wolf Rock and thence to Trevose Head, to a distance of ten miles off the coast. Further patches moving slowly eastwards. Wreck of *Torrey Canyon* breaking up and all vessels advised to give wide berth.

ELEVENTH DAY

09.20   T.H.V. *Stella* commenced towing Seven Stones Lightvessel towards Penzance.

08.03   Information from Inspector that the Navy will attempt to set fire to oil slick west of Lizard. Authorities informed.

09.08   Information from H.M.S. *Wooten* that helicopter will use Very lights to indicate oil patches.

15.00   Information received that eight 'Buccaneer' aircraft will bomb wreck at 15.45. Local authorities and Lloyd's London informed.

15.15   Bombing commenced. Third bomb scored hit and set wreck on fire.

17.25   Further attacks by 'Hunter' aircraft from Chivenor using drop tanks to further ignite oil.

Oil Situation: Oil extends round coastline from Trevose Head to Lizard. Coastal pollution: most beaches Trevose Head to Land's End badly affected. Beaches on east side Land's End peninsular fairly clear.

TWELFTH DAY

12.20   Tanker again bombed and set on fire. Further bombing took place during afternoon.

Oil Situation: Oil extending fifteen miles off shore Hartland Point to Lizard, mostly thin but thicker patches in places. Coastal pollution: All beaches affected from west of Trevose Head to Land's End – mainly thick oil.

Oil reports will continue to be passed to authorities concerned until further instructions are received.'

During the *Torrey Canyon* emergency Land's End Radio Station handled nearly two hundred ship-to-shore radio-telephone calls totalling 21½ hours, and this did not include free medical advice calls between the tanker and a mainland hospital.

Detergents used in the cleaning-up operation totalled 6,740 tons at £100 a ton – the tanker's cargo of crude oil was insured for less – £436,000.

One bright spot amidst the filth that polluted the coast was the rescue of an eleven year old boy who fell off a cliff at Cape Cornwall. He fractured both legs but the fact that he was not killed was due, in part, to a pool of thick oil which choked the small inlet and cushioned his fall. He was rescued by Coastguard Cliff Rescue Company men from St Just.

14
Afloat Again

All maritime nations have Coastguard organizations of varying size and complexity, but the most elaborate is that of the United States in America.

The U.S. Coast Guard, a para-naval force was 180 years old in August 1970. In the 1960s while carrying out its traditional role of guardian of life and property at sea, the ships of the service helped to fight the sea war against the Communists in Vietnam.

Mr H. R. Kaplin, in an article published in 1968, recorded that in 1967 the Coast Guard reinforced its coastal surveillance of the South Vietnamese waters by dispatching five 311-foot ocean-going cutters to this area, to supplement twenty-six eighty-two foot cutters which had been on patrol duty in south-east Asia since 1965.

The Squadron had its headquarters in Subic Bay, Republic of the Philippines and, in two years of activity had inspected and boarded over 252,000 junks, taken into custody 226 suspicious looking native craft and 4,188 persons suspected of assisting the enemy.

Cutters on patrol duty provided gunfire support for allied forces ashore, and often shot it out with enemy craft. 119 Viet Cong craft were destroyed, including steel-hulled vessels heavily laden with materials destined for the war fronts.

Besides maintaining coastal surveillance the U.S. Coast Guard in Vietnam carried out port safety functions, handled merchant marine personnel problems, supervised the loading of explosives and other dangerous cargoes, and maintained aids to navigation.

Nearly 1,500 Coast Guardsmen were on duty in Vietnam in 1967, out of a total force of 36,000.

In general, as the principal U.S. agency for promoting safety at sea, the Coast Guard maintains a diversified maritime safety programme designed to prevent disasters at sea and, to carry out quick and effective search and rescue operations when they do happen. The cornerstone of the preventive safety programme is the Coast Guard intensive vessel inspection system under which every U.S. vessel subject to inspection laws is placed under scrutiny from the blueprint stage throughout its operating life.

In 1967 the programme involved some 9,253 commercial vessels.

The ships, aircraft and small boats of the service answered 42,000 calls for assistance in 1967 and saved more than 3,000 lives, while assisting nearly 127,00 persons.

The value of property involved totalled some $2,859,698,000. Contributing to the search and rescue effort is the Coast Guard Automated Merchant Vessel Reporting System which, through its computer centre in New York City, plotted the location of some 1,000 ships in the Atlantic Ocean and 800 in the Pacific each day. This pinpointing of precise ship location assists the Coast Guard in providing the fastest possible response when disaster strikes on the high seas.

The U.S. Coast Guard's concern for safety on the water, like the British service, includes the millions of recreational craft. This is largely entrusted to the Boating Safety Division which carries out a programme of safety education and law enforcement. Under the authority of the Federal Boating Act 1958 the Coast Guard entered into agreements with ten States for law enforcement and patrolling of regattas.

Forty mobile boarding units were employed for safety patrols, examination of boats, and public safety education.

In 1967 a vicious hurricane 'Beulah' in three days of fury in Texas flooded the Rio Grande. Working round the clock the Coast Guard helicopters evacuated hundreds of people from the stricken areas. Food and water were airlifted to the flooded sections and every available Coast Guard helicopter was pressed into service.

The International Ice Patrol which the U.S. Coast Guard has been operating since 1914 in the North Atlantic protects shipping against floating ice hazards.

Plans for replacing the Coast Guard's ageing fleet went ahead in 1967. Two of a new class 378-foot high-endurance cutters were commissioned and five others were launched.

Two 210-foot medium-endurance cutters were commissioned

and four were launched, bringing the total number of these craft in service to seven, with nine others in various stages of construction.

1967 was also an important year for Coast Guard aviation. Amphibious turbine-powered helicopters replaced the last of the piston-powered machines at Air Station Traverse City, Michigan, and a new air station was under construction.

The men of the British Coastguard are not, however, envious of their American counterpart. Their history has proved that as a life-saving organization their place is on the land round the coasts, and not as an adjunct to the Royal Navy.

To take to the sea again, except in specific life-saving roles, would be to squander the vast storehouse of knowledge reposing in the modern Coastguards, which can be seen from the requirements set down in Coastguard Regulations, 1966, which state that members of the Service are not allowed to join the Royal Fleet Reserve, or other reserve forces, and are required to resign therefrom, on appointment to H.M. Coastguard.

To become a Coastguardsman, applicants must satisfy examiners that they have an adequate knowledge of:

1. The basis of the Coastguard organization, and the part played by the Coastguard Auxiliary Service. The various categories of Stations, and the methods used for setting watch.

   The procedure for setting bad or thick weather or special watch, when the weather conditions or other circumstances require it.

   The communication system normally employed at Coastguard Stations; priority for life-saving messages sent by telephone. The methods prescribed for the passing of distress information to stations if the telephone is not available.

2. The Search and Rescue organization and the various authorities associated with it.

   The action taken at a Post Office Coast Radio Station and at Coastguard Stations on the receipt of a distress message from a ship at sea.

   The procedure for informing the R.N.L.I. and rescue helicopters of casualties; the responsibility for the launching of the lifeboat and calling out rescue helicopters. The liaison between Coastguard and Ministry of Defence (Navy) and (Air) and the procedure for obtaining assistance of ships, aircraft and helicopters when this is necessary.

The 'sunken submarine' instructions and the part played in them by the Coastguard.

The action taken by Coastguard when fishing vessels and other vessels are reported missing or overdue.

The procedure for initiating and co-ordinating search and rescue measures for service or civil aircraft casualties.

3. The radius of action of lifeboats including Inshore Rescue boats.

The radio equipment carried by lifeboats and the methods and procedure used for communication between them and the Coastguard.

4. The operational capabilities of rescue aircraft and helicopters, and the communications equipment carried on them.

5. Knowledge of the Merchant Shipping Act as it affects Coastguard when they are acting for the Receiver of Wreck.

The duties of a British Sea Fishery Officer and the action to be taken against encroachment by foreign fishing vessels. The method of obtaining the position of a vessel which is suspected of illegal fishing. The action to be taken when a fisherman reports damage to his nets.

The responsibilities of the Coastguard in connection with the foreshore, and with the illegal removal of sand and gravel.

The action to be taken by Coastguard when oil pollution is seen or reported to them.

6. The ability to send and read messages made in morse, by lamp, and in semaphore by flags, at the rate of six and ten words per minute respectively.

Voice procedure for transmitting and receiving messages and operation of Coastguard radio sets.

The International Code of Signals; the shape and colour of all the alphabetical flags and their meaning when flown.

The statutory distress signals for vessels and aircraft

and the other signals often made by vessels to indicate distress and, the replies made from the shore to indicate that they have been seen.

The signals employed in connection with the use of Coastguard rescue equipment, and the signals for 'Warning off' any vessel seen to be standing into danger.

The lights and shapes carried by every type of vessel at sea, at anchor, and when aground in or near a fairway and, the sound signals made by all such vessels.

7. Knowledge of Coastguard rescue equipment, ability to rig and handle the gear, deal with breakdowns and, cliff rescues. The ability to make thirteen knots including splices, whipping bowlines and clove hitch. The ability to demonstrate the line-throwing equipment, the use of cliff lines and cliff ladders, and the use of the helicopter strop.

Restoration of the apparently drowned by mouth-to-mouth respiratory and, external cardiac methods of resuscitation. Methods of landing a boat on an open beach through surf.

Identification of vessels by their rig or other features.

8. Ability to read charts and to plot a position. To fix a position from cross-bearings, calculate the direction and rate of tide using Admiralty charts and tide-tables, and of the drift due to wind, of a disabled vessel or of a rubber inflatable raft and, the interpretation of these calculations for passing to lifeboats, helicopters or other rescue aircraft or vessels.

The colour and shape of buoys used as navigational marks. The characteristics of all the local lights shown from, or fog signals made by, lighthouses, lightships or buoys, and of any local navigational dangers. The best landing places for boats, and any locality dangerous to bathers. The rate and direction of the tidal stream off the local coastline.

The local cliff-paths, by-ways, etc. suitable for the transportation of the Coastguard Rescue Equipment to the beach, and where to obtain doctors, police, telephones, motor transport, local boats or helicopters.

9. The local duties of the Coastguard in relation to or on

behalf of: Ministry of Defence (Navy) and (Air); Lloyd's;
H.M. Customs and Excise; Ministry of Public Buildings
and Works; Trinity House or other Lighthouse Authorities; Society for the Protection of Wild Birds and other
Societies.

All this specialized knowledge is necessary to carry out the
duties of H.M. Coastguard as the authority responsible for
initiating and co-ordinating the civil search and rescue measures
for all ships in distress off the coasts of the United Kingdom.
The area over which this responsibility extends approximates to
that which can be reached by long-range aircraft capable of
operating up to 1,000 miles from the shore.

Liaison is also maintained with foreign search and rescue
authorities.

In 1970 the Coastguard Service was organized in ten divisions, each divided into three districts controlled by District
Officers based at Coastguard Rescue Headquarters.

There were 127 Coastguard Stations manned by regular Coastguards and 245 auxiliary Stations. There were 500 regular personnel and 7,000 part-time auxiliaries, most of whom were members of the Coastguard Rescue Companies which manned the
breeches buoy and other rescue equipment, and carried out
searches along the coast when required.

With the changing pattern of emergencies at sea, the night
watch at some stations was abolished in 1969, but forty-eight
stations maintained constant watch – thirty-one of them being
the Coastguard Rescue Headquarters, and the remaining seventeen where there was a large volume of coastal and fishing traffic
or exceptional hazards.

Intermediate stations kept watch during predictably busy times
of the day and in bad weather. Radio watch was kept on a special
VHF Coastguard-R.N.L.I.-helicopter channel, and the radio-
telephone distress frequency was monitored. Information of a
casualty was circulated by 'telex' and telephone. The '999' emergency telephone service was extended in coastal areas to cover
calls from the Coastguard as well as police, fire and ambulance.

A Committee to review the Marine Search and Rescue Organization of the U.K., which met under the chairmanship of the
Board of Trade, with members from the Ministry of Defence,

Post Office, other Government Departments, the R.N.L.I. and merchant navy associations reported in 1970.

The Committee stated that the U.K. arrangements for marine search and rescue worked extremely well, and made no recommendations for drastic change.

The increase in pleasure sailing and motor-boating produced more calls on the rescue services – the Coastguard handled 1,030 small boat incidents in 1968 compared with 429 in 1964 and, the total number of incidents, excluding false alarms was 2,039 in 1968 compared with 929 in 1964.

But the Committee stated 'These calls have been met and we do not think that there is a need to set up in this country any national marine rescue organization on the lines of the U.S. Coast Guard to bring together all aspects of marine search and rescue.'

The men of H.M. Coastguard are not complacent, they have many ideas for revolutionizing the service in the 1970s. They visualize the number of Coastguard Rescue H.Q.s being reduced, but those remaining would become more important operations centres, on the lines of the modern police H.Q. These would have an incident room receiving '999' emergency calls and issuing orders to two-man, radio controlled, Coastguard vehicles on constant patrol along the coasts. These patrols would be equipped with emergency life-saving gear and, possibly, a type of inshore rescue boat which could be launched if necessary immediately the patrol reached the scene of an incident.

The help of the public living on the coast would be enlisted to report anything unusual or suspicious, in the same way as they would dial '999' for the police.

There would be fewer fixed look-outs, except those overlooking busy sea lanes. The Coastguard Divisions would be freed from much central 'red tape' and given much more responsibility.

Responsible yachtsmen and fishermen might be recruited into a special Auxiliary Coastguard Service and supplied with Coastguard radio sets for keeping a listening watch on a distress wavelength. They would report the names and positions of vessels in their vicinity that could be called to assist in a rescue operation. This would reduce the need to launch lifeboats for casualties occurring a long distance from the shore.

Closer integration with the R.N.L.I. to produce a viable, meaningful liaison is considered necessary, so that lifeboat stations could be moved to take into account the ever-changing pattern of marine traffic. To give the Coastguard the right to call out the lifeboat instead of the cumbersome system which at present requires the Hon Secretary of the local R.N.L.I. to be contacted and his permission obtained before the Coastguard can fire a maroon to call the lifeboat crew.

While these are visions for the future, one innovation was announced in 1970.

Charles Kingsley once wrote 'But men must work and women must weep, Though storms be sudden and waters deep.'

The Board of Trade changed all that with an announcement that the recruitment of women into the Auxiliary Coastguard had been authorized. Lieut. Commander John Douglas, M.B.E., R.N.(Retd.), Chief Inspector of Coastguard enumerated the qualifications for women who could join at sixteen years: good sight for look-out duty; intelligence for alerting the right services in time of crisis, and routing of rescue craft. Cool heads for dealing with incoherent telephone callers; clear voices for relaying vital information; and stamina to stand long hours during rescue operations.

The women were being recruited to work in look-outs, operations rooms and communications. 'We don't envisage women doing heavy stuff like breeches buoy rescues or going over cliffs', said the Commander, 'we want them to do the sort of thing a woman would think of first . . . like standing by with hot drinks and blankets ready for the returning rescuers.'

For the Coastguard and the country the wheel has come full circle. As in the bad old days of the seventeenth century there is no one organization responsible for preventing landings on our shores and, although smugglers no longer land huge masses of illicit goods, the modern freetrader has turned to equally profitable merchandise, the smuggling of Indian and Pakistani nationals in contravention of the immigration regulations.

The Coastguard being a life-saving organization is not required to watch for such landings, although a suspicious craft seen from a look-out would be reported to the police.

H.M. Customs & Excise confine their activities in the main to ports of entry, and what supervision there is in coastal areas

198

is just one of the many responsibilities of the already over-worked and undermanned police forces.

The police do call upon the Coastguard to help them search for clues if illicit landings are suspected to have occurred.

This happened at Whitsun 1970 when a report reached the authorities that a German vessel with a cargo of illegal immigrants was cruising off the Aberdeenshire coast and, a convoy of cars and a lorry was rumoured to be travelling north to an unknown rendezvous. For forty-eight hours police from north-east Scotland as far south as Durham, with the help of the Coastguard and the Auxiliary Coastguards, searched every sandy cove for tell-tale footprints, but nothing was found, nor was anything heard of the fate of the immigrants who may or may not have been landed.

The Coastguards of the 1970s will emulate their forebears by once more going to sea, but not as in the past in support of the Revenue. They will be protecting British trawlers, operating off Iceland in winter, from the weather.

The *Miranda* was purchased by the Board of Trade in 1969 for trawler support duties. This followed the loss of three British trawlers the *St Romanus*, *Kingston Peridot* and *Ross Cleveland* in February 1968 – a major disaster to the fishing industry. There was great public concern that these vessels had gone down in north-easterly storms which were described by experienced seamen as the worst for fifty years. There were severe icing conditions and it was thought that the weight of ice which formed on the superstructures and rigging caused the trawlers to capsize.

Discussions between the Government and the fishing industry took place within days of the disaster and Commander Douglas, then Deputy Chief Inspector of Coastguard was sent as Control Officer to the British weather ship *Weather Reporter* which was moved 100 miles north of her station. The control officer advised trawler skippers to leave the area and seek shelter when the weather reports indicated danger from icing and storms.

Following the success of this emergency arrangement the *Orsino* a modern stern trawler was chartered as a Weather Advisory Ship from 1st December 1968 to 30th April 1969 and again 1st December 1969 to 30th April 1970. She was stationed in the sea area north of Iceland and maintained regular radio contact with all British trawlers fishing north of latitude 61 degrees N, checking their positions and giving weather forecasts and advice on the safety of the vessels.

The *Orsino* also provided a day-to-day medical service with a doctor giving radio advice and visiting sick and injured men in the trawlers. Treatment was provided in the ship's sick bay.

In the winter of 1968-69 the *Orsino* spent 154 days at sea and travelled 6,210 miles. She issued 189 gale and icing warnings, sent 3,104 signals and received 5,580, made 298 position checks on trawlers sailing between the U.K. and Iceland.

During the five months, trawlers fishing in the area made 243 voyages, and the daily average off Iceland was eighteen.

The doctor made sixty visits to trawlers to attend sick fishermen, using an inflatable dinghy, and transferred forty men to the sick bay of the *Orsino*.

In the following winter the *Orsino* covered 17,459 miles. She issued 118 gale warnings and thirty-five severe icing and storm warnings. 7,000 radio messages were handled and advice to trawler skippers to leave the fishing grounds and seek shelter was given on sixteen occasions.

The number of trawlers fishing in the area averaged twenty-nine daily.

A pattern of safety was built up by radio contact between the ship and H.M. Coastguard Rescue Headquarters, Gorleston, Norfolk. The movement of 50-60 trawlers was checked daily and their progress plotted. Radio checks were made with the trawlers and any discrepancies in numbers investigated. Search and rescue operations were initiated when necessary.

District Inspectors of the Coastguard went in turn to the ship for a tour of duty as Weather Advisory Officer.

The two-year experiment was successful and the Board of Trade then bought the *Miranda*, Swedish built of about 1,000 tons at a cost of £90,000. She had been specially strengthened against ice and was converted to carry the latest meteorological and radio equipment, a well equipped hospital, and quarters for a meteorologist, doctor, sick berth attendant and sufficient radio officers to provide continuous communication with the fishing fleet and the home stations.

The ship commanded by an officer of the Coastguard had a crew of Coastguards once more going to sea wearing the Coastguard uniform.

In one other field the British Coastguard is likely to emulate their U.S. counterpart.

The withdrawal of R.A.F. helicopters from Manston, Kent in 1969 and from Chivenor in 1972 which would leave large areas of the coasts of Southern England devoid of helicopter cover at instant readiness was considered by the Committee on Search and Rescue which recommended that the Government should examine the possibility of making civil funds available for the operation of Search and Rescue Helicopters where there was no adequate coverage by military aircraft.

The Board of Trade called for a report which was produced in July 1970.

If the Government provides the necessary cash the familiar petty-officer uniform of H.M. Coastguard may yet be seen in the skies above our coasts.

As the sea becomes an ever more popular playground the calls on the rescue services of the Coastguard will inevitably increase, and the cost of these services will, if history repeats itself, be called into question.

The Committee estimated that at least £4 million was spent every year on civil marine search and rescue, and suggested that there might be a case for passing some of the burden from the tax-payer to those who benefit more directly from these services.

The Committee's final conclusion may well foretell the future. 'As more and more people put to sea in small boats, there is a constant need for training and educating them, and it may eventually become necessary to consider some method to restrain those who would otherwise make a call on the rescue services through foolhardiness.'

H.M. Coastguard already carry out the training and education whenever they are given the opportunity, and, if restraint of the foolhardy ever becomes necessary, the history of the service suggests that this will inevitably be one more item added to the miscellaneous duties of this great organization.

Index

Admiralty; accepted Coast Blockade plan 35; Coastguard transferred to 68; Coastguard Instructions 85; considered Blockade success 36; general memorandum on recruiting 56; issued Consolidation Order 43; Regulations for Coastguard 49; transfer of cruisers 32, 41; Coastguard, cost to 95; Coastguard attitude to 100; Minute on state of Coastguard Stations 106; plan for redistribution of Coastguard 128

Agriculture, Board of 96; Ministry of 129

Air Observer Posts 164

Air/sea Rescue service 164, 167

Alderney, smugglers of 30

AMELIE, French lugger 77

ANSON H.M.S., frigate 91

ARGUS, Revenue cruiser 66

ASHANTI, H.M.S. 163

Auckland, Earl of 59

Auxilliary Coastguard Service 86, 161; armed forces of Crown 165

Bailey, E. C., Coastguardsman 175

Baker, Henry, supervisor, on smuggling 20; on riding officers 26

Ballinagall Coastguard Station, attacked 118, 120

Ballyglass Coastguard Station, burned 126

Ballyheigue Coastguard Station, burned 121

Batten, Major, J. P. for Sussex 23

Battledress, Khaki, Coastguards issued with 165

Bedingfeld, Captain 71

Belderig Coastguard Station, evacuated 124

Belford, Northumberland 161

Bell, Sergeant John 89

Bempton, cliff rescue company 177

Beresford, Admiral Lord 133

Berwick upon Tweed, rescue rocket fired 93, 173; Inshore Rescue boat 178

Birkbeck, Sir Edward 81

Black, G. A. coastguardsman 172

BLENHEIM H.M.S. 70

Blockade Stations 35

Blyth, life-saving company 143

Boatmen, commissioned, duties of 34

Bowen, Frank 110, 112

Boy Scouts, coastwatching scouts 108, 115

Boys, Admiral 76

Boxer, Capt Edward Mourrier 91

Brailey, Surgeon-Captain A. R. 147

Brand, Lieutenant Charles 38

Brandon Quay Coastguard Station, attacked 119; destroyed 120

Bribery 52

BRISTOL, CITY OF barque 88

Buckle, Captain C. 71

Buoys, beacons, light vessels, Coastguard report on 69

CADMUS, H.M.S. 78

CAIRNGORM, M/V wrecked 163

Cameron Highlanders, guarded coastguard station 126

Channel Islands 30

Channel Squadron 73

CHARLES, SS wrecked 144

Charlton Forest 23

Chater, Fordingbridge shoemaker 23, 24, 25

Chichester Assizes 25

Chief Inspector, 143, reports 155, 157, 162, 164, 166, 167, 198

Chief Officers, i/c stations 33; mates appointed 62

Civil aviation rescue organization 156

Civilian officers, appointment of 37, 62

Clarendon, Earl of 66

CLYDE, LORD H.M.S. 72
Coast Blockade 30, 35, 37, 38, 43; broken up 47; assessment of 56
Coast defence, Coastguard proposed for 58
Coast communications 81, 96
Coastguard, H.M. formation 35; official title 43; chain of command 43; pay 46, 49; cost 50, 63; uniform 62; recruiting 62; squadron 70; Act, parliamentary debate 65; Act 68; new Act 138; regulations 193; armed 163; New Force 113; orders, telephone duties 82; signal stations 81, 83; Stations 35; ranks changed 106; Rescue H.Q. 196; reorganisation 94; work of 95; wartime organization of 165
Coast Life-saving Corps 153, 161
Coast searcher 165
Collusion 52, 55
Comptroller-General 38, 47
Corbett: *History of Great War: Naval Operations* 109
Cornish Coastguard records 51
CORNWALLIS, H.M.S. 70
Couch, *History of Polperro* 37
CRESSY, H.M.S. sinking of 109
Crimean War 64; Coastguard drafted 65; Revenue Cruisers 65
Crouch's 'Complete Guide' 39
Cullercoats, volunteer life brigade 88
Customs, H.M., ineffectual 20; new equipment 26; Outport records 27, 28; waterguard under 31; Consolidation Order 43; Select Committee on 63; oppose Coastguard transfer 67; Departmental Committee on Coastguard 94
Custom House sloops 39

Daintree, Captain J. D. 144
Daly, M. Customs examining officer 69
Deal, Kent, houses closed 37; Coastguards cautioned against abduction 53
'D' day, warnings to Coastguard 166
de Chair, Admiral Sir Dudley 108, 114
Deputy Chief Inspector 143
DEVENTIA, SS wrecked 145
Diggle, Lieutenant-Colonel John 147

Dingle Bay coastguard station 120
Donkeys 63
Douglas, Commander John 198
Dunkirk, smugglers' port 20; distillery 30;

EAGLE, H.M.S. 71
Eastbourne, threat to blockade officer at 38
East Grinstead assizes 25
East India Company, tea smuggling report 21
ELIZABETH, brig 90
Eugene, Prince 27
Excisemen, targets for attack 21

Fairall, William, smuggler 25
FAMA, Prussian barque 67
FAME, H.M.S. 163
Farquhar, Vice-Admiral Arthur M. 107
Fenit coastguard station attacked 121
Fetter Lane 25
Fighting gangs 54
Flamborough Head cliff rescue company 177
Flogging 36
Folkestone, coastguard records 54; donkey orders 63
Fordingbridge clue to gang at 23
Foreland, North and South 35
FORMIDABLE, H.M.S. torpedoed 109
Fort Halstead 92
Fortnightly Review 133
Fremantle, Sir Edmund R. 71
Fremantle, Sir Thomas 68
FROIJA, Russian barque 66

Galley, tidewaiter 23, 24, 25
GANYMEDE, H.M.S. 35
Geddes axe 131
German Imperial Fleet, Coastguards died fighting 108
Glan Bay coastguard station, evacuation of 124
Glazebrook, Captain R.C. 147
Gobby ships 72
Gorleston Coastguard Rescue H.Q. 200
Goudhurst Militia 22
Graham, Sir Jas. 47
Grandy, Commander S. W. 66

Gravelines, smugglers' camp at 20
Great gun exercise, inspection 59
Guernsey, smugglers in 30; Royal
   Courts of 30

Hardy, Sir Thomas Masterman 36
Harris' Well, Ladyholt Park 24
HASTINGS, H.M.S. 71
HAWKE, H.M.S. sunk 109
Hawkhurst Gang 22, 23, 25
Hay, Lord John 73
Helicopters 201
Henderson, Admiral Sir Reginald
   100
Heppel, District Officer George 173
HOGUE, H.M.S. sinking of 109
Holland, tea smuggling from 21
Holt, Vice-Admiral R. V. 162
Holy Island 161
Hope, Admiral Sir George 151
Hope Cove Life-saving company 145
Horsham, smugglers executed at 25
Hughes, Commander H. M. 121, 123
Hughes, Commander John 67
Hydrographer, reports to 134
HYPERION, H.M.S. 36

Import duties 41
IMPULSE, schooner 88
Inland Revenue, Select Committee
   on 68
Inquiry, Commissioner of 41
Inshore Rescue Boat 178
Inspecting Captains appointed 31
Inspecting Commanders appointed
   33; reports to 36
Interdepartmental Conference on
   Coastguard 97 100; report adopted
   138
Ireland Coastguard in 117; stations
   destroyed 117; attacks on stations
   118-127
Ireland waterguard 32
ISLANDER loss of 140, 146; Court
   of Inquiry 149

Jack and ensign to wear 40
JEANNE GOUGY wrecked 178
Jerningham Commander 59
JOHANNES Russian brigantine 67
JOHNS, THOMAS H.M. Trawler
   124
Johnson, Station Officer C. H. 176

KAMSCHATKA, Russian barque 66
Kaplin, H. R. 191
Kennington, William, coastguard 126
Key, Admiral Sir Cooper 73, 76
King, Commodore H. Douglas, M.P.
   147
King George V approved Coast-
   guard Long Service Medal 143
King, I. T., Auxilliary Coastguard
Kingsmill, Thomas, smuggler 22, 25
   108
KINGSTON PERIDOT, loss of 199

Land smugglers 21
Lantivet Bay 148
LAURENCE, steamer wrecked 143
Lepper, Lieutenant CWVTS 124
Lewty, Commander J. J. 92
Libraries for Coastguard 62
Lifeboats, Coastguards to take part
   in 69; number of 97
Lifesaving apparatus first mentioned
   33
Lifesaving duties of Coastguard 96
Lifesaving rockets issued 64
Lindisfarne Castle 161
LION, Revenue cruiser 67
LIVONIA, Russian brig 66
Lloyds of London, signalling for 83;
   payments 85; Committee of 134
London dangerous place 31
Long Service Medal 143
Lympne aircraft emergency service
   156

Malinmore coastguard station burned
   124
Man Isle of 177
Manby, George William 89
Marine Search and Rescue Com-
   mittee 196
Marlborough, Duke of 27
Marque, letters of 40
Martello Towers 35
Martin, Rear-Admiral W. E. R. 138
McCullough, Capt. Jock 34, 35
Mercantile Marine Division, Board
   of Trade 140
Merchant Shipping Act 85
MERWEDE, SS wrecked 146
MIRANDA, Coastguard support
   ship 199, 200
Mobilization 40

Index

Modern equipment for coastguard stations 172
Monthly Intelligence 26
Mounted guard, reorganization of 49; pay of 50

Napier, Sir Charles 65
Napoleon, Emperor 19
National Expenditure, Committee on 131
National Service Scheme 161
Naval Coast Volunteers 61
Naval and Military Gazette 59
Naval protective guard 35
Naval Staff Conference on Coastguard 114, 115, 132
Naval War Signal Stations 156
Newgate Prison 25
Newhaven lifesaving company 146
North Berwick life-saving company 144

Observer Corps, Royal, exercises 156, 164 167
ORSINO, chartered trawler 199
Outport Records, Customs 27

PALMER, ALEXANDER, H.M. Trawler 124
Pakenham, Lord 66
Payne, widow 23
Peach, Station Officer R. J. 176
PEMBROKE, H.M.S. 70
Pensions introduced 63
PETREL, revenue cruiser 66
Phipps, William, riding officer 27
Pistol firing, coastguard practice 106
Plant, G. A. volunteer-in-charge 176
Polruan Coastguard Station 149
Poole, raid on Customs House 23
Port Signal Stations 111
Port William, smuggling centre 55
Post Office telegraphic system 81
PRESIDENT II, H.M.S. 162
Preventive Waterguard established 27; duties 31; transfer to Treasury 32; Districts 31; duties of 37; Consolidation Order 43; withdrawn 36

Quiller-Couch, Sir Arthur 150

Radar, use of 167

Rake, near Liss 24
RAMILLIES, H.M.S. 36
Ramsbottom, Captain R. 176
RASK, coaster wrecked 173
Rescue Rocket 92, 173
Revenue Cruisers 33; crews of 37; work of 38; discipline 41; Consolidation Order 43
Revenue Cutter Service developed 36
Rewards, division of 39, 45
Rice, Admiral Sir Ernest 83, 94
Riding Officers, targets for attacks 21; troops assisted 26; establishment reduced 27; waterguard to supplement 31; Consolidation Order 43; disappeared 50
Robertson, Edmund 99
Rocket life-saving apparatus 89; companies responsible for 85
Roker life-saving brigade 163
Roseveare Ralph 147
ROSS CLEVELAND loss of 199
Rowley, Sir Charles 91
Royal National Lifeboat Association 81
Royal National Lifeboat Institution, Select Committee on 98
Royal Navy, Coastguard as a Reserve 58, 97, 112

Salvage, first payment of 56
'Saved' picture inspired by rescue 87
Schiedam, gin distillery 30
Scotland, waterguard established 32
Seahouses life-saving company 175
Seamines coastguard defused 110
Searle, Commander Sidney 147
Sea smugglers 21
SERENE, H.M.S. 124
SEVERN, H.M.S. 35
Shaw, Hon. Henry 44
Sheerness, wireless telegraphy station 111
Shipminder, London 140; codeword 160
Shore Naval Telegraph Stations 104
Signal exercises 81
Sinclair, Miss Alexandra 162
Sinn Fein attacked Coastguard Station 126
Skipwith, Commander Grey 66
Sloops, instructions to captains of 39
SNIPE, brig 90

206

Society for the Encouragement of Arts, Manufactures & Commerce 89
South Shields volunteer life brigade 86, 163
Sparshott, Commander Samuel 61
ST. ROMANUS, loss off 199
Stanstead, White Hart Inn 23
Stewart, Captain Houston 59
Sussex Advertiser 50

Tea smuggling 21, 31
Teelin Coastguard Station attacked 126
TENTERDEN, schooner 86
Thursby, Admiral Sir Cecil 137
Timblick, Chief Officer George 125
Tobacco smuggling 32
Tobacco trade, Select Committee on 63
TORREY CANYON 179-190
Torr Head Coastguard Station raided 125; evacuated 126
Trade, Board of 85; assumed control of coastguard 138; policy for coastguard 140, 142; war instructions 159
Treasury, H.M. transfer of revenue cruisers to 32; Minute 40; transfer of coastguard to Admiralty, Minute 49; refusal to accept Coastguard Conference 102
Trengrouse, Henry 90
Trinity House Elder Bretheren of 134
Tupper Admiral 117

Tyne Improvement Commission 87
Tynemouth volunteer life brigade 86

Union Jack Club, Coastguard families evacuated to 127
URCHIN H.M.S. 121
U.S. Coast Guard 191-193

VALKYRIE, H.M.S. 124
Volunteer Life-saving Brigades 86

Wallis, Coastguardsman R. 180
WARDEN, LORD, H.M.S. 71
War plan, Coastguards 1914 107
War Signal Stations 81, 84, 111
War Watching Organisation 157, 161
Watchmen, London seized smugglers 31
Waterguard, rewards 32
WEATHER REPORTER, weather ship 199
Wennigen, Lieutenant-Commander U-boat 109
Western Approaches, C-in-C 117, 119, 121
Winchester Quarter Sessions 29
Woods, Sir Charles 61, 64
Wool, exportation of 26, 31
World War II, coastguard strength 155
Wreck Service Shield 143
Wrecks, Commission of Inquiry 64

Zeeland, tea smuggling from 21
Zeppelin raids 111